Opera

D0864144

Josef Tichatchek, the first Tannhäuser (Royal Opera House Archives)

Preface

This series, published under the auspices of English National Opera and The Royal Opera, aims to prepare audiences to evaluate and enjoy opera in performance. Each book contains the complete text, set out in this case in transliteration, beside a modern English performing translation. The introductory essays, illustrations and musical analysis have been chosen to focus attention on some of the points of special interest in each work. We hope that, as companions to the opera should be, they are well-informed, witty and attractive.

Nicholas John
Series Editor

Tannhäuser

Richard Wagner

Opera Guides
Series Editor
Nicholas John

OVERTURE

Overture Publishing
an imprint of

ONEWORLD CLASSICS
London House
243-253 Lower Mortlake Road
Richmond
Surrey TW9 2LL
United Kingdom

This Opera Guide first published by John Calder (Publishers) Ltd in 1988

This new edition of *Tannhäuser* Opera Guide first published by Overture
Publishing, an imprint of Oneworld Classics Ltd, in 2011

Printed in the United Kingdom

Contents

List of Illustrations

Cover design: Anita Boyd
Frontispiece: Joseph Tichatchek, the first Tannhäuser (Royal Opera House Archives)

Picture research: Henrietta Bredin

'Tannhäuser' — An Obsession

Mike Ashman

June 1845, letter to Karl Gaillard
I enclose with this letter a copy of my *Tannhäuser* — as he lives and breathes, a German from head to toe.[1]

November 1851, 'A Communication to My Friends'
This Tannhäuser was (. . .) the spirit of the whole Ghibelline race for all ages, represented by one clearly defined and infinitely moving figure; moreover he was a *human being*, a man for today, a man to touch the heart of an artist who longed for real life.

October 1859, letter to Mathilde Wesendonck
Tannhäuser (. . .) the opera in which I first worked with a growing sense of the beautiful and convincing need for transitions.

September 1860, 'Music of the Future'
As to the difference between my *Tannhäuser* and conventional opera, I draw your attention to the *dramatic poem* on which it is based (. . .) although the story deals with legendary miracles, it contains a logical dramatic development (. . .) and makes absolutely no concession to the banal requirements of an opera libretto.

November 1877, Cosima Wagner's Diaries
R. says he has in mind shortening the new first scene considerably, it weighs the rest down too much, there is a lack of balance, this scene goes beyond the style of *Tannhäuser* as a whole (. . .) The problem occupies him greatly.

March 1881, letter to Ludwig II
Recently Rubinstein (. . .) played us the first scene of *Tannhäuser* (. . .) [it] far surpasses anything that even Berlioz achieved in this dissolute genre and (. . .) it is certainly not inferior to anything that I myself have written.

February 1883, Cosima Wagner's Diaries
He also declares his wish to do *Tannhäuser* in Bayreuth first; he says that if he can get this settled, he will have achieved more than by staging *Tristan*.

Tannhäuser is unique among Wagner's dramas. It may be considered as his only large-scale unfinished work; yet, paradoxically, it exists in four stages of completion (one of them in a 'foreign' language) which could be performed as musical entities. I take these to be: what was performed at the first night in Dresden, 1845; the published score of 1860; a choice of material offered at the three Paris performances of 1861, in French; and the Vienna 'version'

1. Translations in this article are: for Wagner's letters, *Selected Letters of Richard Wagner*, translated and edited by Stewart Spencer and Barry Millington (Dent); for Cosima Wagner's *Diaries*, Geoffrey Skelton (Collins); for *Mein Leben*, Andrew Gray, edited by Mary Whittall (Cambridge); and for Wagner's essays, W. Ashton Ellis, slightly adapted. In this Guide, unless otherwise credited, quotations from the *Tannhäuser* text are from Rodney Blumer's performing translation.

supervised by Wagner in 1875. Ever the practical man of the theatre, Wagner was prepared to accept and make often astonishing cuts and transpositions — consider the Munich *Dutchman* performances of 1864 — but he rarely revised earlier compositions wholesale. *Tannhäuser* is the major exception. A full list of changes, which began the day after the Dresden première of October 1845 and continued until the performances in Vienna in November 1875, would number over 30 items — including the addition of whole new scenes and the translation of the entire libretto into French. Every time Wagner was directly involved with mounting the work, he changed it, often on a performance to performance basis. In Dresden between 1845 and 1848 alone he performed two different endings, three versions of the Act Three prelude and at least three versions of the Shepherd Boy's cor anglais solo. In Paris in 1861 none of the three evenings had an identical musical text. *Tannhäuser* was also the only score which he submitted to the full 19th-century operatic treadmill of a gala opening in Paris. And lastly, although prolific with the pen about all his stage works and their reception, Wagner wrote more about the actual performing of *Tannhäuser* than about any other of his dramas.

So why this obsession? The circumstances of the work's creation made it inevitable that it would become an *oeuvre à clef*, a major piece of experimentation and also a kind of 'Portrait of Dorian Grey' which had to be continually retouched as its author matured. *Tannhäuser* was the first major work principally conceived during Wagner's residence in Dresden — a schizophrenic period of relative security and nascent fame as regards his material existence but of major upheaval and revolutionary anticipation in his artistic life. The subject — and the musical material — of *Tannhäuser* clearly mirror this schizophrenia. In less than seven years, Wagner effectively planned his entire life's work: *Dutchman*, *Tannhäuser* and *Lohengrin* were written; the dramas of *The Ring* and *The Mastersingers* sketched in outline; and *Tristan* and *Parsifal* 'researched' and mentally filed. In later life it was always *Tannhäuser* that Wagner cited as the major stepping stone of his development. In 1860, introducing his 'new' *Tristan* music to Paris, he described the step he took from then contemporary opera to *Tannhäuser* as 'mein erster Standpunkt' ('my first standpoint'). In 1882 he told Cosima that '*Tannhäuser*, *Tristan* and *Parsifal* belong together' and called the earliest work 'a consummate drama . . . [with] musically some things insufficiently expressed'.

At the time he wrote *Tannhäuser* Wagner had access to all the tools of the working dramatic composer — a stage, musicians and singers, and commissions to put on his own works. The Dresden period was, in practice, his equivalent of Verdi's 'galley years': he *had* to compose, and to produce work at a speed that often outstripped his capabilities. 'At the time that I wrote *Tannhäuser*,' he wrote to Mathilde Wesendonck in April 1860, 'I was not yet able to do the sort of thing that is necessary here [i.e. for the new Venusberg scene] (. . .) only now that I have written Isolde's final transfiguration have I been able to find the right ending for the *Flying Dutchman* overture as well as — the horrors of the Venusberg. One becomes all-powerful only by playing with the world.' In the 1850s, in enforced exile in Switzerland, without a company to hand or any sign of prospective performances which he could personally control, Wagner the musician significantly fell silent and written theory preceded experiment. *Tannhäuser* was, and had to be, an experiment in music *sur le vif*; for that reason it was never perfected to his satisfaction.

Heinrich Knote as Tannhäuser in 1908 (Royal Opera House Archives)

Dramatically, the work is a Janus-faced cornucopia of its composer's obsessions. This 'consummate drama' has renunciations, a curse, a *Liebestod*, a redemption, a singing competition and magical transformations of both scenery and stage properties. Wagner would later create whole dramas out of just one of these embryo strands: the examination of the social function and subject matter of art in *The Mastersingers*, the renunciation of love in *The Ring*, or the longing for a state beyond mortal existence in *Tristan*.

These themes were not merely prefigured in *Tannhäuser* but were continually reworked — at source, so to speak — whenever *Tannhäuser* was revised. The score was like an artist's drawing board for experiment. Material was 'borrowed' but frequently repaid with interest. In Paris, for example, the score was given the chromatic clothing that turned Venus from the one-scene operatic devil of Dresden in 1845 into a major character representing the pull of selfish erotic love — the polar opposite of the 'pure' love of Elisabeth.[2] But

2. Ironically, for the second (and third) performances in Paris, Wagner was forced to make two cuts in this new duet and, because of problems with the stage band, to omit the second appearance of Venus altogether.

in this reworking of the Act One Venus / Tannhäuser duet, words and music began to anticipate the Parsifal / Kundry confrontation of the 1880s. The 'hero' escapes the 'temptress' at a terrible price: his freedom is illusory. Another instance of experimentation was how the ambivalence surrounding Elisabeth's *Liebestod* was resolved — in Dresden her body appeared onstage for the finale. That he was obviously still uneasy with this[3] may be judged from the fact that he never again wrote a dramatic conclusion provoked simply by a *Liebestod*: Isolde is 'transfigured', Brünnhilde (after much textual revision) immolates herself.

This market in ideas drawn from the *Tannhäuser* scenario extends also to the autobiographical — or, perhaps, fictional-biographical — element in the work itself. The idea that Tannhäuser himself represents the artist in society ('a man for today, a man to touch the heart of an artist who longed for real life') is a controversial one, as capable of upsetting a Bayreuth audience in the 1970s as much as Wagner's stage audience in the Wartburg.[4] Yet it seems central to an understanding of the piece and lies at the heart both of Wagner's feeling that he had made no 'concessions' to the paraphernalia of traditional opera and of his difficulties with interpreters of the title role. Wagner's autobiographical writing contains many a colourful reinterpretation of the placing of his stage works in a life scheme that he was consciously (and retrospectively) inventing. Even allowing for such licence, it is interesting that just six years after the première of *Tannhäuser* he was making extensive parallels in the essay *A Communication to My Friends* between his life in art and the events befalling his last three stage heroes. As the Dutchman is shunned by a materialist, contemporary society for the 'crime' of hubris and for holding to a vision of faithful love, and Lohengrin's right to be a kind of 'tone-poet seer', who must reveal the truth in his own time, is fatally questioned, so Tannhäuser is initially rejected and condemned for attempting to introduce 'worldly' experience into the rarified and abstract atmosphere of the minstrels' art.

Compare the following passages. In the first of his verses to Venus, Tannhäuser tells her: *lit.* 'My heart yearned for pleasure (. . .) you were gracious enough to give to me, a mortal, what you once gave only to the gods (. . .) but your love is too much for me (. . .) I am subject to change (. . .) my heart doesn't just want pleasure (. . .) in the midst of joy I long for suffering.'

3. In August 1853 Wagner instructed Louis Schindelmeisser in Wiesbaden that 'the corpse of Elisabeth does *not* appear, neither do the Landgrave and minstrels . . . Elisabeth's death is indicated only by the light of torches on the Wartburg, funeral bells and men's voices . . . prosaic calculations about the socio-physico-anatomical possibility of burying Elisabeth "in so short a space of time" (how fortunate that people have time on these occasions to think about time!) have finally sickened me to such an extent that I have decided on *this* alteration, or restitution'. The corpse made an official reappearance in later versions of the work . . .

4. Götz Friedrich's epoch-making production opened in Bayreuth in 1972. It showed Tannhäuser as the artist-outsider in a predominantly hostile (and militaristic) Wartburg society, had the roles of Venus and Elisabeth doubled, and (at least at the first performances) had the final chorus performed in contemporary dress. Particular exception was taken to the violent reaction of the knights and minstrels to Tannhäuser's 'blasphemy' in Act Two — but such a reaction was specifically asked for by Wagner. This staging not only opened the way to the 'new' New Bayreuth style of Chéreau and Kupfer but wrote *finis* to an era of imitation-Wieland Wagner productions worldwide.

Milka Ternina as Elisabeth in 1901 (Royal Opera House Archives)

These lines already appear in the first Dresden version of the score.

In *A Communication*, Wagner told his would-be disciples about his mental state in 1844/45: 'The sense of physical comfort which stole over me in consequence of the turn-around in my material fortunes, and grew into a pleasurable feeling of self-content through my first taste of a settled position in life — and especially of public favour and admiration — soon betrayed me into a growing repudiation and abuse of my inner nature.' Later, noting that he was heading down 'a path which, as an artist, must soon bitterly disgust me', he identified a way-out: 'a double revolt of man and artist which

11

The Hall of Song in Wolfgang Wagner's production at Bayreuth, 1987 (photo: Lauterwasser, Festspielleitung Bayreuth)

inevitably took on the form of a yearning for appeasement in a higher, nobler element (. . .) a pure, chaste, virginal, ungraspable and unapproachable ideal of love (. . .) a longing for release from the present, for (. . .) a love denied on earth and reachable through the gates of death alone.'

In the Paris extension of the scene, Tannhäuser tells Venus: 'My yearning drives me on towards some struggle. I do not seek joy and pleasure (. . .) I am driven to look for death.' Then, in both versions of the score, he escapes with the phrase, 'Mein Heil liegt in Maria!' (*lit.* 'My salvation lies with Maria' — the Virgin Mary), rejecting a self-indulgent love for 'pure' love (to be represented by Elisabeth).

If Wagner was Tannhäuser, Tannhäuser is now Wagner — even if the essay is almost as fictional as the libretto. Although the Parisian verses were written after Wagner had read Schopenhauer, it is remarkable how the earlier libretto anticipates Wagner's obsession with life and love beyond death. The dramaturgy of *Tannhäuser* may appear naive — saint versus sinner, sex versus salvation. Wagner himself hinted as much with his remark that a glimpse of a beautiful picture of the Virgin Mary could turn a man away from lustful thoughts of Venus without his necessarily embracing piety. In *A Communication to My Friends*, Wagner poured scorn on critics who 'insist on reading into my *Tannhäuser* a specifically Christian and impotently pietestic drift'. Its simple dramatic structure may best be explained in that, before the final version of the end of *Götterdämmerung* and the conception of *Parsifal*, he handled the battle between good and evil in an overtly black and white manner, redolent of contemporary grand opera.

From autobiographical recreation to the reality of theatrical staging Wagner's obsession continued. He soon realised that his central figure was more than the conventional operatic knight trapped in the morality of a medieval world. Here was both a 20th-century psychological hero and a truly 1840s romantic hero, whose battles took place in his mind. The original ending — without Venus or Elisabeth but merely some lighting effects — is astonishingly and daringly modern. Wagner quickly made the changes to it that conventional stage practice demanded. But the text, or rather the importance that the text carried in the work, he could and would not change. This 'modern' hero soliloquised at some length — and mostly without conventional musical support or decoration. Wagner notes in *My Life* how his first (and less than successful) Venus, his idol Wilhelmine Schroeder-Devrient, identified the problem clearly during a mid-rehearsal visit: 'she (. . .) read the principal passages of the last Act with great beauty and emotion, only to ask me how in the world I could possible expect such a childish fellow as Tichatschek [the first Rienzi and Tannhäuser] to find the necessary nuances for this Tannhäuser. I tried to murmur something to her about the nature of my music and how it was exact enough to compel the singer to express the necessary accentuations (. . .).'

The problem did not go away. After the first night, Wagner was forced to make three cuts in Tannhäuser's part — one of them admittedly stemming from the inadequacy of Venus herself — and, more importantly, to embark on several lengthy explanations of why making just one of these — the passage in the Act Two finale beginning 'Zum Heil den Sündigen zu führen' ('to lead the sinner to salvation') — was tantamount to losing the entire meaning of the role.

The Hall of Song in the 1970 production by Hans-Peter Lehmann, designed by Rudolph Heinrich, choreographer John Cranko at the Bayerische Staatsoper, Munich (photo: Rudolf Betz)

In 1852, in his essay *On Performing 'Tannhäuser'*, Wagner explained: 'Tannhaüser — terribly moved by Elisabeth's intervention (. . .) and the awareness of his hideous blasphemy against her — has fallen to the ground (. . .) in utter humiliation (. . .) these words ['Zum Heil . . .' et seq] (. . .) comprise the very nerve of the events which will befall Tannhäuser in the future and are the crux of his whole existence (. . .) if we are not eventually led here to feel the deepest compassion for him (. . .) even the recital of his sufferings in the Third Act can never compensate us for this lost impression.'

By the time the score was published for the first time (1860) Wagner had hit upon the idea of making this a solo passage for the tenor. At rehearsals in Paris this was not enough for the 'coward who runs around whining loudly that he is ruining his voice with my *Tannhäuser*'. The 'coward' was Albert Niemann whom Wagner in a long letter (ironically interrupted by a message from the tenor threatening to resign if this passage were not cut) exhorted: 'throw yourself into it body and soul, as though you did not have another note to sing after this finale.'

That, however, was principally a vocal problem. In Paris Wagner spoke about the Third Act 'recital' attempting to explain away the difficulties (predicted by Schroeder-Devrient) which arose from such a new musical form — an exploratory blending of recitative, *arioso* and *preghiera* which marks the beginning of a more mature musico-dramatic style. 'I find you far too fresh', wrote the composer/producer to Niemann, 'I do not *want* an exhibition of sensual vocal strength (. . .) if I wanted to keep pace with you, I should have to rescore the entire orchestral accompaniment at your entrance. Everything here is calculated to produce a ghostly tonelessness which gradually rises to the level of a touching tenderness but no further.[5] There is too much physical strength in your rendering of the narration up to your arrival in Rome: that is not how a man would speak who had just been roused from madness to a few minutes' lucidity, a being from whom others shy away when they meet him, who for months has gone almost entirely without food (. . .) even if Tannhäuser were to be somewhat hoarse in the Third Act, this would be no great misfortune (. . .)'. And he repeats the warning: 'you should not sacrifice the passage in the Second Act finale for the sake of this one here.'

It is hard to imagine how new these simple and moving acting instructions —note, incidentally, the parallels between his description of Tannhäuser's mental state and Siegmund's in Act One of the 1854 *Valkyrie* — must have seemed in 1861, let alone in 1852 when Wagner distributed his first thoughts about performing *Tannhäuser*. His initial enthusiasm for the Paris project was based on the apparent chance 'to command the services of the entire institute, just as I think fit' (letter to Julie Ritter); but more than a hundred rehearsals could not inspire a routinely inaccurate conductor or stamp out the habits of bad singers. In his essay of 1852 he had thought it necessary to advise the conductor to read the libretto and the stage directions, the producer to look at the score and to encourage the two to work together as a team (!). He also

5. Minna Wagner was among the first to doubt Wagner's new orchestral style! During rehearsals at Dresden she 'missed the trumpets and trombones that resounded everywhere in *Rienzi* with inexhaustible brilliance' (*Mein Leben*). From Paris she lamented in a letter to her daughter that 'Richard has . . . cut the lovely overture of his *Tannhäuser* and instead has added a mass of Venus hocuspocus'.

recommended that, prior to music rehearsals, 'the poem shall be gone through in the fashion usual with a spoken play, each individual reading his role aloud' and that choral passages 'are to be recited by either the chorus director himself or one of the chorus leaders.' This interesting (and expensive) idea is not yet widely practised in the world's opera houses.

Wagner embraced wholeheartedly the radical idea of naturalistic staging: 'If the entry of the guests into the Singers' Hall be so effected that the choir and supers march upon the stage in double file, draw the favourite serpentine curve around it, and take possession of the wings like two regiments of well-drilled troops in wait for further operatic business — then I merely beg the band to play some march from *Norma* or *Belisario* but not my music (. . .) the more varied and unconstrained are the groups of oncomers, divided into separate knots of friends or relatives, the more attractive will be the effect of the whole Entry.' He went on to ask for similar realism in the entry of the pilgrims in both Acts and in the choreography for the Bacchanale.[6] Further pamphlets — *Staging Tannhäuser* and *A Description of the Costumes*, distributed in handwritten copies after the Dresden première — call for the use of child supers to mime the distant approach of the pilgrims and the departure of Elisabeth towards the Wartburg in Act Three. There are also virtually cue by cue descriptions of the major stage transformations in Acts One and Three. For the mid-19th century this production book detail is quite remarkable.

Wagner's obsession with *Tannhäuser* stemmed from the fact that he came to use performances of the piece as a working model to gauge his own progress in the craft of writing music drama. The process may have begun because *Tannhäuser* was being widely performed in the 1850s in Germany but it certainly continued because Wagner saw that the work was something of a lexicon of ideas, both musical and dramatic, that were to inform and dominate nis future output. In 1859 — preparing the first published score, which was to be almost immediately obsolete — he 'canonised' *Tannhäuser* by calling it 'Handlung' (drama), the title he used for *Tristan*. Today's problem with editions, which is often glibly summarised as a choice between the 'Dresden' version (meaning really the revisions collected up until 1860 in that first published score) and the 'Paris' version (meaning really the subsequent Munich and Vienna revisions), would have been anathema to Wagner: for him, *Tannhäuser* was, quite simply, its latest current edition. When Cosima first staged the work at Bayreuth in 1891 she talked of 'a battle of life and death between opera and drama'. It was this battle that Wagner was determined to win by his obsessive revisions to the score.

6. The extended Paris Bacchanale was Wagner's compromise answer to the Opéra's demands for a ballet in Act Two to appease local taste. Curiously, Wagner's final work *Parsifal* not only virtually complies with Parisian taste by having a big number for 'les girls' in Act Two — the Flowermaiden scene being a sort of 'ballet chanté' — but calls for processions that probably should 'take possession of the wings like two regiments of well-drilled troops'.

Lauritz Melchior as Tannhäuser and Elisabeth Rethberg as Elisabeth, San Francisco, 1934 (photo: Morton)

Tanhusære, Danheüser and Tannhäuser

Stewart Spencer

The historical Tanhusære is believed to have been a Franconian knight from the village of Thannhausen to the south-west of Nuremberg. Like many of the land-hungry, adventure-seeking barons of his day, he may have taken part in a Crusade to the Holy Land, perhaps setting sail from Apulia in January 1228 with the Emperor Frederick II and returning the following year. His knowledge of Cyprus suggests that he joined the expedition there in 1231-33, a foray which may also have taken him to Antioch and southern Turkey. A brief appointment at the Court of King Henry VII (who reigned 1220-35) was soon followed by a longer one with Frederick II of Babenberg (1230-46). Frederick's premature death in battle against the Hungarians brought an end to the poet's years of prosperity, and the remaining third of his life was spent in a peripatetic quest for a new patron. He died shortly after 1266.

In one of his songs written after the death of Duke Frederick II, the poet lists the four types of theme he would celebrate if a new patron were to offer him an appointment at Court:

How well I'd sing, and better far,	ich sunge wol und verre baz
of all the women fair.	von allen frouwen schoene.
I'd sing of heath and open fields,	Ich sunge von der heide,
of trees and of the May,	von loube und von dem meien,
I'd sing of summer, and of dance	ich sunge von der sumerzit,
and of the roundelay;	von tanze und ouch von reien;
I'd sing of freezing snow and rain,	ich sunge von dem kalden sne,
and of the winter wind,	von regen und von winde,
I'd sing of father and of mother,	ich sunge von dem vater,
and of infantkind.	von der muoter und dem kinde.

Sixteen of Der Tanhusære's songs have survived in the early fourteenth-century Heidelberg (Manesse) Manuscript, and they all centre upon these four traditional themes. The treatment which they are accorded could be described as epigonal rather than innovatory. Der Tanhusære was writing at the end of the period of so-called classical Middle High German literature, at a time when the contemplative ideal of an inspirational and unconsummated love had long since ceased to provide poetic inspiration. In condemning its exaggerated demands, Der Tanhusære was only one of a long series of critics stretching back at least as far as the beginning of the century, when Wolfram von Eschenbach had ridiculed the lady's extravagant claims on her lover's patience and prowess in the figure of Orgeluse. Der Tanhusære's lyrics depict an overtly sexual relationship pursued in dance rhythms and consummated in the open meadow. But however rustic the setting, the women whom he described (in notably intimate detail) conform to the courtly ideal of feminine beauty.

It is not clear whether the final line of the strophe quoted above refers to the geneaology of royal houses (the subject of two of the poet's surviving *Leiche*) or to more spiritual matters. Although doubts have been raised as to the authenticity of a penitential hymn ascribed to 'Der tanvser' (i.e. Der Tanhusære) in the mid-fourteenth-century Jena Manuscript, there would be nothing unusual if a poet of the earlier century had struck this general note of *memento mori* and asked for remission of his non-specific sins. The *Busslied* has

The Heidelberg Codex illustration of 'Der Tanhuser'

plenty of literary precedents, and any attempt to read personalised sentiments into literary attitudes is bound to appear an anachronistic exercise for a time when the majority of artists were content to remain anonymous and the concept of individuality in art was still to be coined. (Our own poet, after all, is simply 'the man from Thannhausen'.) In sum, there is nothing in the poet's life or works to connect him with the legend which later grew up around his name.

The same is true of the illustration in the Heidelberg Codex depicting 'Der Tanhuser' as a member of the Teutonic Order of Knights. The cloak he is seen wearing is the sort of civilian dress that a Crusader might have worn, certainly not the pilgrim's penitential rags. And, in spite of attempts to claim otherwise, neither the poet's self-consciously frontal stance nor the figural design to either side of him can be related to the Danheüser of the Ballad or to the pope's burgeoning staff, since both have too many iconographical parallels elsewhere in the manuscript. (It may be noted that the Heidelberg Codex miniatures did inspire the designs for Siegfried Wagner's 1930 Bayreuth production of *Tannhäuser*.)

We now enter the realm of speculation. No satisfactory account has yet been produced to explain the poet's reappearance in the sixteenth-century *Lied von dem Danheüser* (always assuming the two to be one and the same person, which is itself by no means certain). The following summary is bound to raise as many questions as it seeks to solve.

Das Lied von dem Danheüser first appeared in a printed broad-sheet in 1515 but is known to have existed since at least the 1480s. It tells of Danheüser's

Costume designs by Alfred Albert for the Paris production in 1861: Venus and a chorus 'Seigneur' (photo: Bibliothèque Nationale)

decision to abandon the Venusberg and his mistress's erotic charms, of his journey to Rome in search of absolution, and of the pope's apparent refusal to remit his sins:

The pope was leaning on a staff	Der Babst het ein steblein in der handt,
and it was dry and dead.	Das was sich also dürre:
'This shall have leaves ere you receive	'Als wenig es begrünen mag,
the grace of God,' he said.	Kumpst du zu gottes hulde.'

In his despair Danheüser returns to the Venusberg, and thus fails to catch the latest news: the papal staff had burst into leaf.

Tannhäuser's name had first been amorously associated with that of Venus in Hermann von Sachsenheim's *Die Mörin (The Mooress)*, a 6000-line epic first printed in Strasbourg in 1512 but surviving in six manuscripts from the middle of the previous century onwards. The poet, Hermann, tells how he was abducted one evening and transported by magic to Venus's island paradise. The goddess arrives (astride an elephant) and accuses him of inconstancy. A trial ensues in which Hermann is represented by Trusty Eckhart and Venus by the mooress of the title, who bears the impossibly incongruous name of Brunhilt. He escapes by reciting the 'Salve regina'. Parading his encyclopædic Renaissance wit and knowledge of medieval texts, the poet turns the crusader Tanhusære into Venus's consort and the northern princess of the *Nibelungenlied* into a Saracen maid. It is not inconceivable that contemporary poets sought to explain Tanhusære's presence at Venus's court by composing the *Lied von dem Danheüser*. In doing so they drew upon an extant tradition associated with the Monte della Sibilla near Norcia in the central Apennines. From around the period 1437-42 comes the account of Antoine de la Sale, who tells how an unnamed German knight had entered the Mountain of the Sybil, succumbed to the Sibyl's blandishments, emerged from the cave, continued his journey to Rome, was refused absolution, and returned to the mountain, never to appear again. La Sale visited the cave himself in 1420 and claims to have heard the story from local villagers.

Meanwhile, in 1440 or thereabouts, Johannes Nider had asked in his *Praeceptorium Divinae Legis* 'whether there be any truth in what they tell about Venus' Mount, where it is said men are to be found living a life of ease and lustful pleasure in company with beautiful women'. This is the first recorded mention of the term Venusberg: the author refers to a place which already exists but whose associations still need to be explained to his readers.[1] Writers anxious to locate the Venusberg naturally fell on the Monte della Sibilla, with the result that Venus came to supplant the Sibyl in later fifteenth-century accounts, to the extent that in 1497 the Curia threatened to excommunicate anyone found in the grotto's precincts. Perhaps predictably, the ban served only to enhance the Venusberg's reputation, in consequence of which it now became, additionally, the fabled seat of necromancy. Not all writers accepted the Italian attribution, and of the fifty or so allusions to the Venusberg which have survived from the fifteenth and sixteenth centuries (the majority unrelated to the figure of Tannhäuser) the greater part of them are non-specific geographically. (The identification of the Venusberg with the Thuringian Hörselberg is not attested before the nineteenth century,

---

1. The medieval view of Venus as a demonic, all-powerful deity stretches back to the second half of the twelfth century, but not until the fifteenth century were she and her retinue housed in a mountain cavern.

Act Two in the 1861 Paris production.

although a pointer may have been provided by Johannes Praetorius's *Blocks-Berges-Verrichtung* of 1668.)

An alternative, ahistorical approach was proposed in 1977 by Dietz-Rüdiger Moser.[2] Moser points out a number of curious features about the Ballad and suggests it had an openly didactic or catechistic purpose. The legend, he argues, ought properly to embody the hero's exemplary progress from repentance to confession and finally to atonement. The nature of the sin — contravention of the vow of chastity[3] — is of such enormity that only the pope can grant absolution. Hence the journey to Rome (which is not itself a pilgrimage) to commune with the appropriate father confessor. The pope declines to offer immediate absolution but offers the sinner a chance to atone, an opportunity which he seizes by returning to the scene of the transgression, the better to confront his sinful nature. The pope's pronouncement is not, therefore, the act of hubris that it must otherwise seem (cf *Matthew* 4:7): the burgeoning staff is a sign of the individual's rebirth following the remission of his sins (cf *John* 3:3). At an early stage, Moser believes, this moral parable was misunderstood, the pope's words being misconstrued as an outright rejection of the penitent reprobate, so that his return to the Venusberg necessarily came to be seen as a relapse into sin. As the Reformation began to gather pace in Germany, the ballad-writer's almost wilfully anti-papal stance inevitably ensured the work's popularity. Whatever the shortcomings of Moser's hypothesis (not least its problems of dating), it has much to recommend it, especially because of the light that it throws on Wagner's libretto.

2. Dietz-Rüdiger Moser, *Die Tannhäuser-Legende: Eine Studie über Intentionalität und Rezeption katechistischer Volkserzählungen zum Buss-Sakrament* (Berlin/New York 1977).

3. Moser proposes this interpretation on the basis of the sixth strophe (lines 21-4) of the Ballad. However, there seems little reason to reject the older view that the hero is guilty of apostasy in worshipping the 'Teüffellinne' or she-devil, Venus.

Wagner himself had been reminded of the legend during his final winter in Paris (1841/2), when his researches into thirteenth-century German history were interrupted by the chance discovery of a certain 'Volksbuch'. In *My Life* the book in question is said to be 'about the Venusberg', whereas the corresponding account in *A Communication to My Friends* insists that the subject matter was Tannhäuser. For a long time both accounts were questioned, and only within the last ten years has it become clear that the book in question was the first volume of Ludwig Bechstein's *Der Sagenschatz und die Sagenkreise des Thüringerlandes* (Hildburghausen 1835). Bechstein reproduces one of the early sixteenth-century printed versions of the *Lied von dem Danheüser* in addition to recounting the legend of St Elisabeth of Hungary (Wagner's Elisabeth) and the tale of Frau Holle in the Hörselberg (Wagner's Frau Holda). But, more importantly, he mistakenly associates the mid-thirteenth-century Tanhusære with the Court of Hermann I of Thuringia, and thus with the Song Contest of 1206/7. This confusion was compounded (and confirmed) for Wagner by his reading of Christoph Theodor Leopold Lucas's *Ueber den Krieg von Wartburg* (Königsberg 1838), in which the author had fancifully claimed that Tannhäuser (aka Heinrich von Ofterdingen) had himself participated in the Wartburg Contest. The way was thus open for Wagner to conflate the two legends, by interpolating the so-called Battle of the Bards between Tannhäuser's departure from the Venusberg and his pilgrimage to Rome. Other poets had already reworked one or other of these legends in the nineteenth century, and although Wagner was later contemptuously dismissive of the 'tendency towards mystical coquettishness and Catholic frivolity' in Ludwig Tieck's *Der getreue Eckart und der Tannenhäuser* and of the 'distortions' of E.T.A. Hoffmann's *Der Kampf der Sänger*, he indisputably helped himself to motifs from both. Other versions with which he was almost certainly familiar include Joseph Eichendorff's *Das Marmorbild* and Heinrich Heine's *Elementargeister*. If Wagner later chose to conceal this debt, it was not so much his proverbial ingratitude or even his reluctance to admit dependence upon a Jew, but because by the 1850s his thinking had been coloured by the *völkisch* ideology of the day: if the musical drama was to be born out of the spirit of the people, then literary precursors must be either ignored or disparaged.

What exactly attracted Wagner to the Tannhäuser Ballad was, by his own account, its 'Germanness'. To a German musician in Paris, suffering financial misery and a sense of alienation from self, the neo-medieval bard must have seemed a kindred spirit. And the role of the artist at odds with society was one which Romantic poets had been prone to assume. None the less, the Tannhäuser legend on its own was not sufficiently dramatic to provide the framework for a three-act opera, and Wagner evidently felt the need to elaborate the plot by adding a further strand. In doing so he risked the displeasure of the more literary members of his audience, for whom the Romantics' preoccupation with the Middle Ages was already growing somewhat tiresome. As early as 1836 Heine had complained of 'this constant obsession with coats of mail, jousting stallions, ladies of the castle, respectable guild-masters, dwarfs, squires, castle chapels, love and religion, and all the rest of your medieval rubbish [. . .]; the German Middle Ages have entered into our midst in broad daylight, and are sucking the life-blood from our breast.' Although Wagner himself did not escape this accusation,[4] he

4. See, for example, Karl Banck's review in the *Dresdner Tageblatt* of September 6, 1846.

Above: Caspar Neher's design for Act Three, Frankfurt, 1934; below: Act One in the 1930s Cologne production produced by Alexander Spring and designed by Alf Björn.

managed to rise above it by relegating the medievalism of the work to mere local colour and by concentrating instead upon a theme which has assured the opera its lasting validity.

'Könnt ihr der Liebe Wesen mir ergründen?' (*lit.* Can you penetrate for me the essence of love?) Landgraf Hermann asks the assembled company in Act Two, and in doing so not only alters the subject matter of the Song Contest, so that the question which the singers address is no longer the praise of princes as in the medieval *Wartburgkrieg* but the nature of love; he also poses a question that was to obsess the composer all his creative life. In *Tannhäuser* the poet answers it equivocally, inasmuch as the hero himself seems in some confusion in the matter of where his real affections lie. If the magic of Elisabeth's name is so potent as to recall him to the Wartburg, what was he doing with Venus in the first place? And why, having forsworn venereal passion, does he then proceed to hymn the goddess's praises in Act Two, and to exhort his astonished listeners to repair straightway to the Venusberg? There is much to be said for the suggestion that the Venusberg is not so much a place as a representation of the hero's sexuality, which he himself is at pains to exorcise, but which may ultimately be exorcisable only through death. On the face of it, the hero's demise is no more necessary than that of Elisabeth herself. The Romantic *Liebestod* of *The Flying Dutchman* strikes one here as somehow out of alignment, an indication of the course that Wagner was shortly to take. The demonic love embodied by the Venusberg (that 'realm of non-being'[5] as the composer was later to call it in a flash of pre-Schopenhauerian insight) is a theme which Wagner had chanced upon while studying the medieval source material; and just as surely as it destroyed both Tannhäuser and Elisabeth, so it will destroy all those of his subsequent characters who cannot learn to transcend it.

5. Programme note written for a performance of the Overture in Zurich on March 16, 1852, reproduced in Attila Csampai and Dietmar Holland (eds), *Richard Wagner: Tannhäuser. Texte, Materialien, Kommentare* (Reinbek bei Hamburg 1986), p. 128.

Wagner's Most Medieval Opera

Timothy McFarland

Although Wagner drew on medieval sources for most of his stage works, *Tannhäuser* is the most medieval of them all. His ability to transform his material, so that it seems to become the expression of central problems and preoccupations of his own Romantic century, is as much in evidence here as anywhere else. But in spite of this the action retains a strikingly medieval character, presenting us with a hero torn between carnal love and spiritual fervour, between pagan sensibility and Christian penance — a hero who appeals to the Virgin Mary to save him, and who is indebted to the intercession of a saint for his ultimate redemption, which is proclaimed to the world by the miracle of a blossoming papal staff. Whether the surviving ballad of Danheüser as printed in 1515 is based upon a moral tale for religious instruction or not[1], it conforms to the general pattern of sin, penance and forgiveness that is dominant in medieval moral narratives, and this remains the basic framework of the opera's action, especially in the final Act.

It also presents us with historical figures of the Middle Ages in a precise location — the court of the Landgrave Hermann of Thuringia at the Wartburg castle near Eisenach — and, with the exception of King Henry the Fowler and the rather shadowy Antwerp of *Lohengrin*, it is the only opera in which Wagner does this. The choice of a specific historical subject matter is, on the other hand, one of the many features which links *Tannhäuser* with *The Mastersingers of Nuremberg*. It has frequently been pointed out that both operas are also about song contests which serve to demonstrate the conflict between the artist and the philistine or un-emancipated society for which he has to perform. In the later, more mature and optimistic work Wagner recreated sixteenth-century Nuremberg as the projection of an ideal German urban community in which the artist could ultimately find an honoured place. No such reconciliation takes place in *Tannhäuser*, however, and the notion of an ideal community is not fully developed. But, as in the later opera, Wagner did choose as his setting a moment of unique symbolic importance in his nation's cultural history. The great lyric poet Walther von der Vogelweide and Wolfram von Eschenbach, the author of *Parzival*, both praised the generosity of Landgrave Hermann as a patron, and they may well have met at his court, although this cannot be proved. (The late thirteenth-century text about the song contest, the so-called *Wartburgkrieg*, celebrates the memory of Hermann as a patron but is otherwise quite unhistorical.)

There is undoubtedly an element of cultural patriotism in Wagner's decision to link the Tannhäuser subject with the Wartburg song contest and to set it so firmly in this historical context. The work took on its final shape in the summer months of 1842, when Wagner had returned to Saxony after the miserable years spent in Paris. This too is a link with *The Mastersingers*, the composition of which he was to take in hand in 1861, on his first return visit to Germany after twelve years of exile; that return was a profoundly disappointing experience which filled him with the desire to recreate an ideal historical Germany on the stage. On the earlier occasion Wagner had arrived in Dresden with the *Tannhäuser* material on his mind, certainly well

---

1. For an account of the hypotnesis put forward by Dietz-Rüdiger Moser see the article by Stewart Spencer in this Guide, p. 21.

acquainted with the stories by Tieck, E.T.A. Hoffmann and Eichendorff which treat the same themes and related motifs, and probably with Heine's remarkable essay *Elementargeister*. This not only contained the ballad (as well as Heine's own parodistic version of it) but also included an extended discussion of the theme of the 'gods in exile', the folklore notion that the divinities of classical antiquity had retired after the victory of Christianity to a place of subterranean exile, from where they continued to oppose the guilt-ridden self-denial and penitential asceticism of the medieval world.[2]

Most of the opera's material had thus been in Wagner's mind for some time, but when he came to write the first prose sketch for the libretto during his summer holiday in Teplitz-Schönau in June 1842, the book which would seem to have been uppermost in his mind was the one which he later referred to in his autobiography as a 'Volksbuch vom *Venusberg*' which he had come across by chance in Paris. This contained a version of the material, he said, which was 'based on the well-known old 'Lied vom *Tannhäuser*'.' It is not at all clear from this formulation that Wagner really wished his readers to believe that he had found a *Volksbuch* in the strict sense of the term, i.e. a sixteenth-century chap-book, treating the subject in a prose version which is otherwise unknown to scholarship. These words could also be taken to refer to a book which we know he did read. This wasn't an old *Volksbuch* at all, but a fairly recent collection of stories and legends about medieval Thuringia by the scholar Ludwig Bechstein. It appeared in four volumes, but Wagner found everything he needed in the first of them. *Die Sagen von Eisenach und der Wartburg, dem Hörseelberg und Reinhardsbrunn* (1835). It was Bechstein who decided, evidently quite arbitrarily, to locate the Venusberg in the Hörseelberg, a mountain near the Wartburg, and he also suggested, again without any foundation in earlier stories, that Tannhäuser may have been on his way to Hermann's court when he was lured away by Venus. The two aspects of Wagner's reading of Bechstein that concern us here are firstly the history of the Wartburg itself, a rich tapestry of incident and legend in the best Romantic manner, and secondly the prominence in this account of Saint Elisabeth, the most famous figure in the castle's medieval history.

It is difficult to recapture today a full sense of the importance of the Wartburg as a historical monument for nineteenth-century Germans. Although it had only been the seat of the princes of Thuringia, and not of kings or emperors, it had seen great events and was certainly the most famous castle in Germany. Its association with the best known medieval poets has already been mentioned, and we shall return to the figure of Saint Elisabeth below. At the end of the Middle Ages, when branches of the Saxon dynasty had inherited most of Thuringia, it played a part in the heroic early phase of the Reformation. When Luther had been outlawed after his famous defiance of the emperor Charles V at the Diet of Worms in April 1521, he was waylaid and abducted by soldiers of his own prince and protector, the Saxon elector Frederick the Wise, and brought to the Wartburg, where he was kept in hiding for several months. While there he began his translation of the New Testament into German. Famous in Lutheran lore are the many anecdotes about his visits in the region, bearded and disguised as Junker Jörg, 'Squire George', and tourists are still shown the stain on the wall of his study where he threw his inkpot at the devil.

2. See Dieter Borchmeyer, 'Venus in Exile. Tannhäuser and the Wartburg Tournament of Song', programme for *Tannhäuser*, Bayreuth Festival 1985, pp. 108-36.

Friedrich Schorr as Tannhäuser, San Francisco, 1931 (photo: Morton)

The castle's association with Luther's struggle for religious freedom was instrumental in turning it into a symbol of the struggle for political freedom by German patriotic liberals of the early nineteenth century. In 1817, the tercentenary of the Reformation, it was the scene of the first major demonstration which brought students together in protest from different German states. Although no political action was envisaged, the event had an enormous resonance and was important enough to alarm the reactionary governments, and from that moment on the Wartburg was a potent ideological symbol of German nationalism. When Wagner wrote *Tannhäuser*, in the decade before the 1848 revolution and about twenty-five years after the Wartburg student demonstration, these political and historical associations were paramount in the public mind.

There is no explicit allusion to this political dimension in Bechstein's history, any more than there is in Wagner's opera. Bechstein includes the anecdotes about Luther, but his concern is primarily a regional one; he organises his stories around locations rather than around heroes, and among these locations the 'queen of Thuringia's castles' has pride of place. There is nevertheless an important, if implicit, connection between the fervour with which Bechstein celebrates the Wartburg and the ideological prominence of the castle at that time. For the Romantic generation, political emancipation was associated with the restoration of ancient greatness, the reassertion of an innate strength to which the venerable stones bore witness. By invoking the spirit of the Wartburg and collecting the stories of its ancient history, Bechstein is re-creating an ancient genre in the spirit of Romantic folk-culture, a similar task to that which the Grimms had performed for the folk-tale and Arnim and Brentano for the folk-song. Although, in Bechstein's case, this is less the *Volksbuch* than the dynastic chronicle, the underlying intention is the same. The anecdotes and legends which collect around a great castle and its rulers are seen as the expression of the people's historical consciousness. As such they constitute an important element in the cultural heritage.

So Wagner was reacting in a truly Romantic way when fired with patriotic enthusiasm by his encounter with Bechstein's book. While there is nothing political or revolutionary about the court of the Landgrave as it appears in the second Act of *Tannhäuser*, there is a strong echo of Bechstein's approach, invoking the spirit of the place, in the major chorus ('Freudig begrüssen wir die edle Halle ...'), in Elizabeth's aria ('Dich teure Halle ...') and the Landgrave's address ('Gar viel und schön ward hier in dieser Halle ...'). It is worth stressing this association in the light of the general tendency to see the Wartburg court in negative terms, as the incarnation of a narrow, convention-bound public, incapable of accepting the artist of genius when his emancipated concept of love collides with their own.

The Wartburg is not, however, only the scene of the song contest; it is also the home of Saint Elisabeth, and it is to this historical and legendary figure that we must now turn in order to consider her transformation into the heroine of Wagner's opera. This transformation is so total that we might be inclined to doubt any link at all beyond the mere name: yet then we would have to ask why Wagner chose this name, and thus to link his character with the best-known person in the Wartburg's history before Luther. She entirely dominates Bechstein's account of the castle's history, in which sixteen out of a total of forty-one chapters are devoted to her, whereas there is only one about the song contest.

Elisabeth (1207-1231) was the daughter-in-law of Landgrave Hermann, not his niece; she was born a princess of Hungary and betrothed in infancy to Hermann's son and heir Ludwig, who became Landgrave in 1217. After his death while on crusade in 1227 Elisabeth, a widow at twenty, left the Wartburg and adopted the religious life. Instead of entering a convent or becoming a recluse, as would have been normal up to that time, she remained in the world and embraced a life of extreme voluntary poverty and devotion to works of charity in the spirit of Saint Francis of Assisi. She was a tertiary, or lay member, of the Franciscan order, and the first person of princely rank to model her way of life on that of the saint, who had died in 1226. The intense contrast between the courtly life of the Wartburg and the self-imposed humility of her widowhood impressed her contemporaries greatly, and she became a symbol of the new mode of lay piety. She was canonised in 1235, a mere four years after her death. The official version of her life, a Latin *Vita* by Dietrich of Apolda, was used as the main source for a German verse *Legend of Saint Elisabeth*, composed around 1300. This also included various legendary stories, which remained current in the following centuries, and which Bechstein drew upon. Among them is the account of how the birth of Elisabeth is foretold from the stars by the magician Klingsor, who has been summoned to the Wartburg in order to participate in the great song contest. Klingsor had made his first literary appearance in Wolfram's *Parzival*, but now he has to do service as a magus who, following on the three in the New Testament, is inspired to prophesy a life lived in imitation of Christ.

The cult of Elisabeth was widespread in Europe, but she remained particularly important for central Germany, not least for dynastic reasons. The princely family of Hesse is directly descended from her, and the various branches of the Saxon house of Wettin also claimed her as an ancestor. Apart from the royal line at Dresden (Wagner's own immediate sovereigns), these branches included the ducal houses of Weimar and of Coburg. It was at the end of his period of service to the Weimar court that Liszt composed his oratorio *The Legend of Saint Elisabeth* (1865), a work that may have influenced his son-in-law's *Parsifal*. Through the Coburg connection Elisabeth also became a patron saint of the British royal family. She appears among the forebears of Prince Albert in the windows of the Albert Memorial Chapel at Windsor, and Sir Alfred Gilbert executed an exquisite statue of her in 1899 as part of his work on the tomb of the Duke of Clarence.

Since the cult of St Elisabeth was still so prominent in the nineteenth century, how are we to explain Wagner's need to appropriate her name and her saintliness for his heroine? In doing so he had to cast aside virtually all the historical and legendary motifs of her story. We know from Wagner's own statements and his sources that Elisabeth was the last of the major characters to take shape in his mind, and when this had happened the outline of the opera was complete, more or less in its final form. It was undoubtedly Bechstein's book which gave him the impulse to take the decisive step to put her into the opera. As with the emphasis on the Wartburg castle, Bechstein's collection provided an integrating factor which enabled Wagner to draw together the various elements into a whole.

Wagner's Elisabeth is presented in two sharply contrasted consecutive stages, and her dramatic intervention in the finale of the second Act to defend Tannhäuser is the pivotal point when she moves from the first to the second — from courtly princess to saint. The historical figure of the saint provides a role model in the third Act, and here only to a limited degree. In fact Wagner

Nelson Eddy as Wolfram, San Francisco, 1934 (photo: Morton)

was drawing on a different model in the second Act, although he was unwilling to acknowledge it. This was the fictional heroine of E.T.A. Hoffmann's *Kampf der Sänger*, the beautiful young widowed countess Mathilde von Falkenstein, the 'star of the court', for whose favours two of the poets participating in the contest are rivals — Wolfram and the tortured, sinister genius Heinrich von Ofterdingen, a clear anticipation of Wagner's Tannhäuser. From Hoffmann Wagner had already borrowed Wolfram's friendly behaviour towards his rival, and the theme of love as the subject of the singing contest. For the constellation of figures in this episode, and therefore for the shaping of the second Act, Wagner's debt to Hoffmann is greater than that to Bechstein.

But the Wartburg song contest is not the only subject of the opera. In deciding to integrate it into a treatment of the story of Tannhäuser and the Venusberg, Wagner was following his own dramatic instinct to create two strongly conflicting worlds and sets of values, and to give these two worlds their own modes of musical expression. The greatness of *Tannhäuser* as an opera resides in the manner in which the composer was able to fashion these two musical worlds and the struggle between them for the soul of the hero. We know that for Wagner the development of the musical thought always proceeded hand in hand with the dramatic shaping of the operas: in the case of *Tannhäuser* he must have perceived the need to underline in every possible way the contrast between the pagan and the Christian, between the underworld grotto and the princely castle, and, as an essential aspect of the conflict, between the two women who embody these worlds for the protagonist. As this conflict between pagan sensuality and the spirituality of Christian self-denial took shape, it furthermore became necessary to find a dramatically adequate counterweight to the figure of Venus. The material which Wagner had taken from Hoffmann and elsewhere for the Wartburg song contest offered nothing that he could use for this purpose. A 'Countess Mathilde' figure was still necessary for the second Act, but she could not fulfil the demands of the overall dramatic plan.

Tannhäuser escapes from the Venusberg by a miracle of divine intervention following his appeal to the Blessed Virgin: 'Mein Heil liegt in Maria!' This feature appears in the original ballad, and must have appealed to Wagner strongly. It is at this point, as has frequently been observed, that we become explicitly aware for the first time in the opera that we are witnessing a restatement of the traditional juxtaposition of Venus and the Virgin Mary as the twin divinities of profane and sacred love — an old theme which had assumed a new urgency for the Romantic generation. The Virgin Mary does indeed provide an adequate counterweight to the goddess Venus on the symbolic level, but Wagner could scarcely bring her onto the stage in person without changing the entire work. What he needed, in order to achieve a satisfactory integration of the Tannhäuser and the Wartburg song contest material, was a figure who could combine the dramatic function of the Countess Mathilde, as presiding beauty of the Wartburg and the real prize of the song contest, with that of the Virgin Mary, as a power antithetical to Venus. He needed, in fact, a Thuringian princess who had become a saint.

This is exactly what he found in Bechstein's book. If he had any qualms about the propriety of making St Elisabeth a character in his opera while totally disregarding the well-known stories of her life, these were swept aside in the summer of 1842 when he saw a painting of the Madonna attributed to

Carlo Dolci in the church at Aussig: 'if *Tannhäuser* had seen it, I could readily understand how it was that he turned away from Venus to Mary without necessarily having been inspired by any great sense of piety. — At all events, I am now firmly set on *Saint Elizabeth*. —', he wrote to his friend Kietz in September. This anecdote makes it clear that Wagner's main concern was with the great symbolic juxtaposition of the two female figures, who represent the conflicting psychological states of the hero.

It was above all the final Act of *Tannhäuser* that benefited from this breakthrough. Although Elisabeth's singing role is limited to her prayer, this is sufficient to establish dramatically the achievement of sainthood through self-denial and suffering, and to reinforce the dominant mood introduced by the pilgrims' chorus and continued in Wolfram's aria. None of this is derived from Wagner's sources; it is the direct consequence of the decision to make the heroine of the opera a saint. This enabled the composer to fashion a final Act capable of holding its own against the powerful projection of Venus in the first Act bachannale, and thus to set up the twin powers whose struggle for the soul of Tannhäuser is given such memorable musical form in the final scene. On the immediate level this scene appears to confirm the heroine's victory: the penitent pilgrim has been forgiven by God, and he dies invoking the intercession of St Elisabeth. But the structure of the medieval moral fable is subverted by the score, even if it is not exactly contradicted. Tannhäuser's 'Rome Narration' is not merely the demonstration of his despair, it is also the musical enactment of the disintegration of his personality. We are not to doubt that the spirit has ultimately triumphed over sensuality, for this is put beyond all question in the last pages of the score by the pilgrims' choruses. We may nevertheless wonder how much of him there is left to save after the destruction wrought by the conflict that we have just seen and heard tearing him apart. This is the modern element in *Tannhäuser*, but in order to achieve it Wagner had to employ the authentically medieval juxtaposition of pagan sensuality and Christian sainthood.

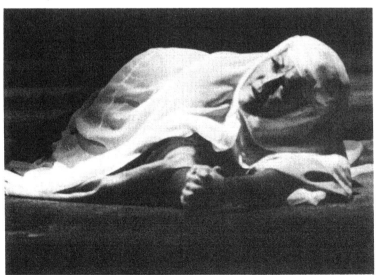

Leonie Rysanek as Elisabeth, San Francisco, 1973 (photo: Ron Scherl)

Orpheus and the Underworld:
The Music of Wagner's 'Tannhäuser'

Carolyn Abbate

R. (. . .) appeared after all to find a certain disproportion between the
new scene and the rest of the piece.
Cosima Wagner's Diaries, October 19, 1881

In the evening some light conversation, which R. finishes off with the
Shepherd's Song from *Tannhäuser*. He says, he still owes *Tannhäuser* to
the world ['er sei der Welt noch den *Tannhäuser* schuldig'].
Cosima Wagner's Diaries, January 23, 1883

What would it have been, the *Tannhäuser* that Wagner owed the world? The
words are disquieting, for we cannot after reading them remain complacent in
our beliefs about masterworks and authorized texts. *Tannhäuser* was the one
work Wagner never perfected and never abandoned. The latest revision of the
opera was that made for the Vienna performances of 1875, and involved some
trivial fixing-up of the radically new version done for Paris in 1861. But the
final version (sometimes called the 'Paris-Vienna' version) was not really
final, or rather it was only made final accidentally, by Wagner's death. The
two remarks cited by Cosima suggest one critical point about this final
version, namely that Wagner recognized a disproportion or imbalance
[Missverhältniss] between the opera's older and newer parts was a defect
needing to be remedied.

Imbalances in *Tannhäuser*, and our knowledge that Wagner himself
recognized them, have combined to make us ambivalent in our attitude
towards the score. *Tannhäuser* has been seen as an unhappy mixture of the
clumsy and the deft, of the banal and the extraordinary. The later Paris-
Vienna version is incongruous, for in it Wagner's new Tristanesque harmonic
and instrumental colour intrudes into a work originally composed in 1843-45.
By 1860, Wagner had left the musical world of German Romanticism and of
German opera. A taste for simple stylistic consistency has led many opera
houses today to perform the standard early version (the 'revised Dresden'
version, finished in 1845 but altered considerably between 1845 and 1849)
despite Wagner's wish, forcefully expressed, that the later revision supercede
it.[1]

But was Wagner's sense of disproportion between the older and newer
layers of the opera necessarily our sense of stylistic inconsistency?
Tannhäuser's two styles can be understood not as a flaw, but as deliberate and
meaningful. The two opposing styles are linked to the dualism of the two
opposed worlds, the realm of Venus and the Wartburg society. The operatic
set pieces, such as the septet in Act One, or the Elisabeth-Tannhäuser duet in
Act Two, are careful and conventional in their prim formality and harmonic

1. Wieland Wagner's production in Bayreuth (1962) favoured a *Tannhäuser* with the
ballet scene (Act One, Scene One) from the Paris revision, but without the coeval Paris
revision of the Tannhäuser-Venus scene (Act One, Scene Two); the old Dresden version
was played instead. This seems perverse; certainly neither of the usual arguments of
'stylistic consistency' (all-Dresden) or 'authority of the composer's last wishes' (Paris-
Vienna) can be adduced in support of the practice.

conservativeness. The radical language of the loosely-organized scenes includes motivic cross-references and odd tonal, harmonic, and rhythmic flourishes: musical prose to the musical poetry of the 'operatic' sections. The ordered society of the Wartburg is thus given a very different musical voice from the Venusberg. What is more, these two different musical voices actually existed from the first, in the original (1845) score; even there, Venus was set apart. Wagner's most important later revisions, undertaken first in spring 1847, when the dénouement of Act Three was recomposed, then in Paris in 1860-61, when both the Bacchanale and the Venus-Tannhäuser scene were recreated, centered upon the scenes in which Venus appears.[2] The Tristanesque Venus of the 1860-61 revision was thus fundamentally the older Dresden Venus, with her radical implications realized in a more forceful way.

I

We need to put aside any prejudices about Venus, whose name in a musical-theatrical context is, perhaps, more suggestive of Offenbachian revels — Zola's Nana in her role of 'la blonde Vénus' — than of Germanic devilry. Though she was partly invented in Paris, and in the French language, Tannhäuser's Venus is not French.[3]

This demonic Venus is the force for disaster in *Tannhäuser*. Though he extricates himself from the underworld, Tannhäuser cannot escape his desire to return. Repeatedly he calls upon Venus at moments of crisis: first, during the Song Contest in Act Two, in rebellion against the platitudinous serenades of the other singers, then in Act Three as a release from the intolerable vision of damnation. When he remembers the Venusberg, he is obliged to relive his experiences of it.

The most famous manifestation of Tannhäuser's compulsion is his outburst in the Song Contest, when he interrupts Wolfram's paean to sacred love by singing the fourth verse of his Song to Venus [8], (the first three verses had been addressed to the goddess in Act One). This compulsion recurs, always involving a similar musical recapitulation. For instance, the cadence to the fourth verse of the Song, 'zieht hin, zieht in den Berg der Venus ein' ('make haste, haste to the Venusberg with me!'), will be repeated in Act Three

2. In the original (1845) version, Venus did not appear on stage or sing at the end of Act Three; instead, her presence and her effect on Tannhäuser were suggested by stage lighting (a red glow in the Hörselberg upstage) and a reference to the Venusberg ballet music from Act One. After seeing the production, Wagner realized that the visual-musical reference was too oblique; the audience was missing the point. In spring 1847 he rewrote the ending; now Venus sang to Tannhäuser, and the demonic world was made manifest.

There were, of course, other important changes that affected the non-Venusian parts of the opera, including two rewritings of the Act Three prelude (one in 1845, one sometime between 1848-52). For a full account of the complex history of *Tannhäuser*'s revisions readers are referred to John Deathridge, Martin Geck, Egon Voss, *Verzeichniss der musakalischen Werke Richard Wagners und ihrer Quellen* (Mainz, 1986), 256-95; the 1860-61 changes are analyzed in Carolyn Abbate, "The 'Parisian' Venus and the 'Paris' *Tannhäuser*", *Journal of American Musicological Society* 36 (Spring 1983), 73-123.

3. The music for her new scene, Act One, Scene Two, was composed to a French text (the only theatre music Wagner ever wrote to a foreign language); the words were only later translated back to the German that now appears in standard editions of the Paris-Vienna version.

34

The Venusberg in Götz Friedrich's Bayreuth production, designed by Jürgen Rose, 1977 (photo: Wilhelm Rauh, Festspielleitung Bayreuth)

as Tannhäuser conjures up his dark mistress, 'nun süsse Göttin, leite mich' ('come to me, Venus, show the way!'), and once again when she appears, 'im Venusberg drangen wie ein' ('the Venusberg enter with me'):[4]

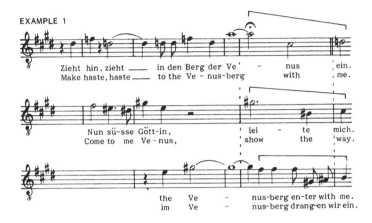

EXAMPLE 1

The motivic fragment — a tiny cadential figure — is cited repeatedly across long stretches of operatic time and within many separate numbers and scenes.

This use of the Song to Venus, quoted from Act One Scene Two as the *coup de théâtre* in the Act Two finale, is an instance of a recurring musical argument. The Song is also used for other special purposes. In itself, it is banal; if Tannhäuser is a Thuringian Orpheus pleading for his own release from Hades, he sorely lacks the eloquence needed to obtain his *congé*. The effect within its larger contexts is far more interesting than the Song itself.

For instance: in Act One Scene Two, the three nearly identical verses — three glorifications of Venus, followed by three pleas for release — are pillars of formal rectitude and musical simplicity: what is more elementary than a strophic song? To be sure, each verse creeps upward by a half-tone (the first is in D♭ major, the second in D, the third in E♭) so though the tenor seems to sing the same music each time, his voice strains perceptibly higher.

Around these verses circle Venus's replies. The idea of interrupting a strophic song with responses has a number of precedents (Osmin's opening *Lied* in *The Seraglio* is one example). Here, however, the verses are separated not by a few remarks, but by longer and longer expanses of music for Venus. This was already true in the Dresden version; for the Paris revision, Wagner completely rewrote her replies, making them even more digressive and elaborate. While the verses of the Song represent a strict, formal backbone, her replies are the opposite. Each is musically unique, each amorphous and unpredictable.

4. Ironically, this cadential fragment appears in the first Act as Tannhäuser's plea for release, 'ach Königin, Göttin, lass mich flieh'n', and his cry to the Virgin at the end of the Venus scene, 'mein Heil liegt in Maria'. The connection is noted by Reinhold Brinkmann, 'Tannhäuser's Lied', in Carl Dahlhaus, ed., *Das Drama Richard Wagners als musikalisches Kunstwerk* (Regensberg, 1970), 199-207.

One extended example must suffice to illustrate the point: the reply to the second verse. Her interruption ('Treuloser? Weh? Was lassest du mich hören' 'Deceiver! Ah, to say this in my hearing!') breaks into a faster tempo, tremolo strings, D minor (to the Song's D major) — all of these musical signs for rage. Tannhäuser joins in — 'Ach, schöne Göttin, wolle mir nicht zürnen' ('Ah, lovely goddess, try to understand me'), but her outburst collapses abruptly into bars of silence broken by diverse musical thoughts, flung out and as quickly abandoned, and finally (in the Paris version) a disorienting, key-less transition:

EXAMPLE 2

Richard Cassilly as Tannhäuser and Jessye Norman as Elisabeth, Covent Garden, 1973

A serene F-major rhapsody will follow [9]. Within this brief space there has been a series of unpredictable shifts from one musical idea to another, between different tonal idioms (diatonic and modulatory/chromatic), between tempi. More than this, there is no attempt to reconcile these juxtaposed statements. They are presented, with deliberation, *apart*; that is the purpose of the odd moments of silence. Her third reply is similar: brief melodic periods [10 and 11, 12] alternate with silences, isolated motifs, musical arguments broken off without warning. In short, her music hints at anarchy. This voice of anarchy engages in a dialogue with the formality and banality of Tannhäuser's Song. That banality is thus part of a larger scheme to divorce Venus's musical discourse both from the rest of the opera and the language of the other characters.

In Act Two, the fourth (E major) verse of the Song has a different sort of role to play. The fourth verse is cast into a long Italianate finale. The Act Two finale follows a typical mid-19th-century pattern, beginning with a recitative and choral introduction (the march and chorus for the guests [20]); a digressive and increasingly tense conversational passage (the Song Contest); a spectacular *coup de théâtre* (here a double one, the Song to Venus [8], and Elisabeth's unexpected defense of Tannhäuser, her piercing 'Haltet ein' 'Stand back!'). The *coup de théâtre* engenders a long *concertato adagio* in reaction to the shock ('ich fleh' für ihn' 'I pray for him' [22] / 'ein Engel stieg aus lichtem Äther' 'From Heaven an angel has descended'); set against this ensemble background is Tannhäuser's voice of remorse.[5] The last part of the finale is prepared by a recitative-like transition: the Landgraf's banishment of Tannhäuser, ('ein fürchtbares Verbrechen' 'A crime against good order'); the final *stretta* follows ('Mit ihnen sollst du wallen' 'Go join them on their journey' [24]). Though Wagner came later to reject the very notion of the Italianate finale as restricting and reactionary, he created in Act Two of *Tannhäuser* one of the century's greatest examples of the genre.

Tannhäuser is prompted to his Song by frustration, pride, and the inescapable memories of Venus. The recurrence of the music not only recalls the episode, it forces the theatre audience to experience something of the emotional *frisson* felt by the stage audience, the Wartburg guests. They do not recognize the Song (since they have not heard it before), and for them mere reference to 'Venus' is enough to engender terror. For the theatre audience, the musical citation shows how memory works and acts as a mnemonic, forcing each listener to envisage Venus and her world with Tannhäuser. Here we are caught up, by means of musical recapitulation, in Wagner's created world.

II

Familiar and prosaic, the Song to Venus is nonetheless tied up with two important musico-dramatic devices in *Tannhäuser*. One is the dualism that separates the world of Venus from Thuringia, and reflects the central oppositions of the drama — pagan and Christian, underworld and upper world, anarchy and order. The other, the recurring music that washes over

5. Wagner wrote that if Tannhäuser is not able to sing above the ensemble, the passage would be debased into ordinariness, and indeed 'have the character of a conventional Adagio ensemble piece, as we are accustomed to hearing in opera finales before the final stretta'. 'Über die Aufführung des *Tannhäusers*,' *Richard Wagner Gesammelte Schriften* (Leipzig, 1871) Vol. V, 123.

the entire opera, is a phenomenon more complicated and idiosyncratic. The recurring ideas are, above all, not leitmotifs in the usual sense.

The dualism of the drama is echoed in musical oppositions of a broad sort, created with a bold hand. Perhaps the broadest is the basic distinction between conventional operatic number and amorphous scene. The opera begins with the latter, the chaos of the long Bacchanale (Act One, Scene One) with its string of musical episodes, and the Venus-Tannhäuser scene, with its dialogue between Venusian flourishes and Tannhäuser's staid formality.

In the Paris revision, the ballet was conceived as a *klassische Walpurgisnacht*, transformed from the lofty Apollonian tone of *Faust II* to the frankly Dionysian: nymphs riot with satyrs and fauns; Amoretti attempt to police them with bow and arrow. In Wagner's original scenario for the Paris revision, there was much more: Maenads, blood sacrifice, tigers, griffons, sphinxes, centaurs — Venus herself finally has to intervene to restore the peace.[6] The original Paris staging — tutu'd and rose-garlanded ballerinas striking poses in *tableaux vivants* — fell short of realizing this alarming programme. The musical material of the Paris Bacchanale is derived in part from motifs present in the Dresden version [1-5, 7], respun in different harmonic combinations and ordered not so much as to please any abstract musical sense as to correspond to specific events in the Dionysian scenario.[7] (Little actual thematic material was new in the 1860-61 revision; [6] is one example.)

The third scene of Act One, following the transformation from the Hörselberg to the Wartburg valley, acts as a transition between the two musical worlds. Scene Three is also magical as it depicts the magic of the upper world, of light and the coming of spring. When the scene opens, the transformation music dissolves upward into the barely audible ranges of violins, and the pit orchestra falls silent. From this moment, we hear no music that does not apparently come from the stage: the shepherd's pipe (infact a cor anglais), the little song he sings [13], the sheep bells, the approaching Pilgrims' chorus [14]. The stage itself has become the progenitor of music.

The orchestral silence is eerie, as if a demonic orchestra for Venus's realm had departed, and will be replaced quietly by an ordinary operatic orchestra, suitable for what is to follow. At the moment Tannhäuser awakes to discover himself transported ('Allmächt'ger dir sei Preis' 'Almighty God be praised!'), the orchestra finds its tongue again, and plays through the reprise of the Pilgrims' chorus as it fades into the distance. As soon as the off-stage hunting horns are heard, the journey to the normal operatic sound world is complete. The Landgraf and the singers bring with them the humanity of the Wartburg society, and the magic in the spring landscape fades. The septet-finale that closes Act One is, like the Act Two finale, of a conventional type; the nervous conversation of the singers and Tannhäuser, which swirls in and out of *arioso* [eg., 15] climaxes as Wolfram calls out 'bleib bei Elisabeth!' ('Stay for Elisabeth!'). The *adagio* [16] is followed by a *stretta* [17] in which the off-stage

6. The scenario was printed in *Richard Wagner: Sämtliche Schriften* (6th edition, Leipzig, 1916), Vol. 11, 414-19.

7. Wagner sketched out a list of events in the scenario, each with its appropriate themes, before he wrote the music. The manuscript is still in the Paris Opéra Library (Opéra rés. A. 604. iii); another copy, belonging to the choreographer Petipa, was printed in the *Journal des Débats* of April 21, 1895, p. 3.

Janis Martin as Venus and Jess Thomas as Tannhäuser in the production by Paul Hager, San Francisco, 1966 (photo: Carolyn Mason Jones)

The Venusberg grotto at Bayreuth, 1892 (Royal Opera House Archives)

hunting horns draw nearer, the whole a Bellini-Meyerbeerian *tour-de-force* raised to a higher Wagnerian power.

Tannhäuser becomes more 'Wartburgian' — more conventionally operatic — during Act One and, as the process continues, reaches a height of formal propriety in Act Two. The second Act is in effect three set pieces, the introductory aria for Elisabeth ('Dich, teu're Halle' 'Great hall of song' [18]), the Elisabeth-Tannhäuser duet ([19], whose excessively 'operatic' character Wagner later denounced), and the finale.[8] In Act Three, whose setting (the Wartburg landscape) parallels that of Act One, the journey is reversed. The 'numbers' (introduction, E♭ major Pilgrims' Chorus [25], Elisabeth's prayer [26], Wolfram's aria 'to the evening star' [27]) give way to a different manner of musical organization. Tannhäuser's Rome Narration, which begins *quasi una aria* [29] but dissolves into Venusian anarchy, is the turning point. Musical discourse begins to change when darkness falls, as the return of Venus is imminent.

The dualism of formality against unconventional amorphousness and rhetorical flourish is only one of the musical oppositions in the score. There is

8. It is interesting that Wagner originally labelled the 'numbers' in the score of *Tannhäuser* in the usual fashion (in his first draft and later orchestral draft for the opera) but suppressed the labels and the division into numbers when making the autograph full score.

a basic tonal dualism as well. The Bacchanale (in both Dresden and Paris-Vienna versions) is in E major, as is the fourth climactic verse of the Song to Venus. In the Act Two finale, that fourth verse comes as a brutal musical interruption of Wolfram's rhapsody to 'hohe Liebe' ('love pure and holy') in E♭ major [21]. When Tannhäuser pushes Wolfram aside, we experience in its purest form an unmediated juxtaposition of these two keys, the chief tonal symbol of the opera. E♭ major is the key of the returning Pilgrims' Chorus in Act Three [25]: it is, of course, the first theme of the 'potpourri' Overture but there in Venus's key of E major. It is also the tonality framing Tannhäuser's vision of a merciful Pope in the Rome Narration ('Und Tausenden er Gnade gab, entsündigt, / er Tausende sich froh erheben hiess' 'and thousands came away that day forgiven, and thousands more were filled with heavenly grace' [30]), and finally the key of the opera's end, of the choruses of redemption, including the Young Pilgrims' annunciation of the miracle in Rome ([31, 30, 32] 'Heil, heil, der Gnade Wunder heil!' 'Praise, praise, give praise to God in Heaven!').

In Act Three, the two opposing tonalities are again put back-to-back, as a symbol of opposing principles. The return of Venus and the Venusberg music appears to move towards a triumph of E major but just at her moment of victory ('nimmer sollst du von mir flieh'n' 'and never seek to leave my side') Wolfram makes an heroic effort, cries out Elisabeth's name, and with his cry wrenches the entire musical argument round to E♭:

EXAMPLE 3

This moment is a deliberate echo of the *coup de théâtre* in the Act One septet-finale, Wolfram's evocation of Elisabeth at another moment of crisis, dissuading Tannhäuser from flight:

EXAMPLE 4

WOLFRAM

Bleib bei E - li - sa - beth!
Stay for E - li - sa - beth!

In Act One, the cry is made in D major, in Act Three it shifts upward a semitone to E♭, in a process similar to the upward transposition of the four verses of Tannhäuser's Song over two Acts from D♭, through D, E♭, reaching the symbolic E major in the end. In both cases, the recurring musical idea is pushed gradually upward to the marked tonality. An arc of tension, engendered by upward transposition, is spun between the nodal points of the repetition, and the repetitions bind up time itself by leading our memory back to what was and connecting it to what we see before us.

III

The recurring musical ideas in *Tannhäuser* have a purpose unlike that they serve in other Wagnerian operas. They represent with few exceptions the conscious memory of a single character, Tannhäuser, and they lay bare the paths and forms taken by his acts of recollection. This is true whether what recurs is a long musical swatch or a fragment. Parts of the G major Pilgrims' Chorus [14a, b, c] recur extensively. When Wolfram refers to the Pilgrims in the first scene of Act Three ('Von Rom zurück erwartet sie die Pilger. Schon fällt das Laub, die Heimkehr steht bevor' 'She waits for those who took the road to Rome'), a phrase from the chorus's opening verse is quoted in the orchestra (one of the rare cases in which music recurs in Tannhäuser's absence and the recurrence comments on the words of another character). The third Act prelude begins as an orchestral re-statement of the entire chorus, which is interrupted between each phrase by other musical ideas. The opening phrase [14a] of the first verse is played as an orchestral choral-prelude under the Landgraf's speech to Tannhäuser near the end of the Act Two finale, advice concerning salvation that refers to the Rome pilgrimage, 'versammelt sind aus meinen Landen' 'a band of many pilgrims has gathered here from far and wide'. In the last moments of the finale's *stretta*, this pilgrims' music makes a far more spectacular entrance. The knights threaten;

Gabriele Schnaut as Venus and Richard Versalle as Tannhäuser, Bayreuth, 1987 (photo: Wilhelm Rauh, Festspielleitung Bayreuth)

the *stretta* builds towards its final cadence (a prolonged hammering on F# in the bass, preparing the final B major chord); but at the moment of resolution the passionless, androgynous voices of the Young Pilgrims float up from the valley [14c]. The key of the chorus, G major, flashes across the F# dominant pedal as an unexpected resolution that is neither false nor illogical. Tannhäuser stands 'transfigured'. He has heard the music before; it woke him in Act One, a veiled enactment of baptism, rebirth, salvation. Here, the music associated with that transcendent moment has reinvoked an aura of hope.

This act of awakening, with its layers of meaning, was a critical moment, and to it accrue many recurring musical symbols; the G major Pilgrims' Chorus, as the music that precipitates Tannhäuser's returning consciousness, is only one of these. When Tannhäuser returns to life he cries out his thanks, 'Allmächt'ger dir sei Preis, / Gross sind die Wunder deiner Gnade' 'Almighty God be praised! Great are the wonders of His mercy!'). The cadential phrase that sets the words appears once more, in his duet with Elisabeth in Act Two, as he explains that a miracle has brought him back to the Wartburg, 'Ein Wunder war's, ein unbegreuflich hohes Wunder' ('A miracle! An unexplained and holy wonder!').

EXAMPLE 5

This musical recurrence in Act Two refers to the instant of Tannhäuser's awakening. When Tannhäuser *himself* awakens: that is critical. The actual miracle, the magical transportation to the upper world as we (the audience) saw and heard it at the beginning of Act One Scene Three, is something which Tannhäuser, unconscious, did not experience and cannot therefore recall. When the orchestra gives us the musical sign for the miracle in Act Two, it remembers not with us but with Tannhäuser. The orchestra is thus not an omniscient narrator, revealing hidden information in leitmotivic asides to the audience. (When the 'Siegfried' motif rings out as Wotan mentions the unknown hero who will brave the fire surrounding Brünnhilde, the orchestra seems to know things the characters can't.) In *Tannhäuser*, by contrast, the orchestra is the sound of Tannhäuser's mind.

Indeed, the music of *Tannhäuser* seems to have little power to recall, to repeat music heard in the past, unless Tannhäuser himself is present on stage, thinking back, remembering. An intimate connection between the protagonist's mind and the opera's music is established in Tannhäuser's first speech:

I dreamed as if I seemed to hear sounds that have been so long denied. I heard a peel of bells so joyfully ringing; Oh, say, how long since I have heard that sound?	Im Traum war mir's als hörte ich — was meinem Ohr so lange fremd, als hörte ich der Glocken frohes Geläute! Oh, sag! Wie lange hört' ich's doch nicht mehr?

Behind his words, the bells ring in the flutes and oboes, E-B-E-B, three times. Wagner paints the dreamy recollections of a recovering amnesiac. As Tannhäuser awakes, all returning past-consciousness is focused first on musical sound. The orchestra does not play an accompaniment or even really a reference, to his words, nor are these real bells tolling. The music is what is inside his mind as he recovers the past.

The intimate connection between music and the hero's conscious memory will be signalled repeatedly — most clearly in Act One, Scene Three, where the orchestra falls silent as Tannhäuser faints and speaks again only when he returns to life. This absence — as a complete lack of music, a silence — is also used in the Rome Narration, when Tannhäuser describes how he sank unconscious after the Pope's curse ('da sank ich in Vernichtung dumpf darieder; die Sinne schwanden mir' 'Then, crushed beneath the weight of condemnation, I fell unconscious.').

During the Song Contest, Tannhäuser reacts oddly to the other singers' offerings, seeming overpowered by a strange spell with 'a sinister smile of the mouth'. He hears the music of the Venus scenes in the orchestra [1, 2, 9]. The past is remembered by its sounds, the music of tumultuous revels [1, 2] and of Venus's voice [9]. When Tannhäuser meets Wolfram while searching for Venus in Act Three, he tries to find her by finding her music. His entrance lines, as he limps out of the darkness, make this explicit:

I heard a human voice.* How sad it sounded, if it were only hers.	Ich hörte Harfenschlag. Wie klang er traurig! — Das kam wohl nicht von ihr.

* [*lit.* the sound of a harp]

What he heard was Wolfram's sad song, and he has followed it to its source. Later, as the Bacchanale music [1-5] floats up from the backstage orchestra, he knows by sound what is near: 'hörst du nicht jubelnde Klänge?' 'Don't you hear jubilant voices?' (*lit.* bells).

The first musical signal of the Wartburg (the bells) unlocks for him a flood of other memories, visual and tactile as well as aural — the sun, the stars, the green of summer, the nightingale. But before anything else happens, it restores his sense of time lost, a consciousness of time which cannot exist without memory:[9]

The time that I have been here,	Die Zeit, die ich hier verweil,
no longer can be measured;	ich kann sie nicht ermessen.
daytime, night-time, mean no more to me.	Tage — Monde — gibt's für mich nicht mehr;

Memory is here unlocked not by a madeleine, as for Proust, but by music; memory gives back to Tannhäuser his sense of time and with it his will to return to the upper world. The bells are the stroke of energy that turns quiescence into action, that sets the drama in motion. Ironically, memory also brings Tannhäuser to grief, and in the end, to his death.

IV

Repeated musical ideas, the opposition of musical formality and amorphousness, Venus's force for disaster, the idea of memory — all the strands are drawn together towards the end of the opera. The third Act, reversing the sequences of the first, moves from the opening procession of introduction, chorus, prayer, aria, to a peripatetic 'scene' that owes nothing to previous conventions for operatic numbers. As Wagner wrote in 1851, 'it was now no longer possible for me to shape my dramatic material to correspond to *a priori* operatic forms (. . .) now the texts of the scene itself would generate a musical setting *sui generis*, appropriate only to that particular scene.'[10]

The Rome Narration in Act Three is the central act of recollection for Tannhäuser. For the on-stage listener, Wolfram, as well as the listeners in the theatre, it is at first a story that explains certain enigmas. Why does Tannhäuser return alone and secretive, at night? What do his torn clothing and odd manner signify? Why does he search again for Venus? The narrative describes a chain of events — the journey to Rome — unknown to Wolfram and the audience alike.

The events of the journey are indeed hidden, although the Act Three prelude, entitled 'Tannhäuser's Pilgrimage', is sometimes supposed to illustrate or represent the journey for the audience. In fact it cannot depict these mysterious events; on the contrary, it is devised to thwart the idea of representation and revelation, to conceal meaning. Certain familiar tunes from the first two Acts appear at the beginning, such as the G major Pilgrims' Chorus [14] and Elisabeth's plea from the Act Two finale [22]. The prelude also toys with the 'Dresden Amen' [30], which Wagner, of course, did not invent (it also appears, for instance, in Mendelssohn's 'Redemption' Symphony), and whose vague associations with Catholicism or salvation were widely recognized. Increasingly, however, the music is not decodable [e.g. 29]: motifs and phrases, calculated to sound portentous, build to a tremendous orchestral climax but are without specific dramatic associations. This is not a literal musical narration but a presentation of musical signifiers that signify nothing. The text ends as undecipherable. The musical elements at the end of the prelude — gloomy, ominous as they are — are left unexplained, and this creates an air of deliberate mystery. The Rome

9. 'What sort of life, what sort of a world . . . can be preserved in a man who has lost the greater part of his memory, and with this, his past, and his moorings in time?' [Oliver Sacks, *The Man Who Mistook His Wife for a Hat* (New York, 1985), p. 22.]

10. 'Eine Mitteilung an meine Freunde', *Richard Wagner: Gesammelte Schriften* (Leipzig, 1871) Vol. IV, 391.

Narration will later clarify the meaning of the Prelude's end, by 'replaying' this end at the same time Tannhäuser's words reveal what happened after the journey to Rome. In this sense, the Act Three Prelude ends with a series of enigmatic gestures, whose meaning, like the 'meaning' of the words in Sherlock Holmes' famous 'Musgrave Ritual' verse, is not clear until a revelatory narration provides the true history behind the enigmatic series, thus solving the mystery.[11]

The Rome Narration unfolds on two levels. First, it recounts Tannhäuser's journey — it depicts the past. At the same time, it represents the protagonist's collapse into madness as he tells the story — it depicts the present. Tannhäuser begins the Narration rather coolly, establishing a formal storytelling situation by requesting Wolfram in recitative to stand clear and listen quietly. The careful recitative that ushers in the Narration signals 'aria' as strongly here as it might in a Mozart opera, and the start of the Narration is almost balladic, using a minor *ostinato* theme [29] to define the opening of each verse ('inbrunst im Herzen' and 'wie neben mir der schwerstbedrückte Pilger'). This strophic formality suggests that the song is a fictional epic — but the tale told here is no fiction.

The formality soon begins to disintegrate as Tannhäuser describes his arrival in Rome and his first sight of the Pope ('nach Rom gelangt ich so zu heiligen Stelle' 'I came at last to Rome, the holy city'). The tonal centre of the opening verses (A minor / F major) and the *ostinato* theme cedes to a wholly new key area (first Db, then Eb) and a new thematic idea, the ecclesiastical sound of the 'Dresden Amen' [30]. The abrupt abandonment of the initial musical argument (the minor strophes, the *ostinato* theme) is symbolic on the narrative level, since it is a musical response to the events of the story, and a representation of Rome with its 'hymns and songs of grace', in sharp contrast to the hardships of the journey. This abrupt musical change also functions on the psychological level. It suggests illogicality, non sequitur; it is the first intimation of a musical-formal collapse.

In the extraordinary final moments of the Narration, as Tannhäuser approaches his memory of the Pope's curse, musical order dissolves into anarchy. With no central key, no sustained thematic periods, the music darts from one symbol to the next in echoing Tannhäuser's memory of diverse events and actions. His slow, limping walk towards the Pope calls up the *ostinato* theme of the Narration's opening [29], his confession an echo of the strings of the Venusberg. The heart of the Narration, the quotation of the Pope's words, is sung to an ugly shard of music [28], a slow, dark, fanfare that outlines the uneasy diminished fifth A-Eb, and that had dogged Tannhäuser's steps in the beginning of the scene ('die Stätte, wo ich raste, ist verflucht' *lit.* the place where I stand is accursed). Tannhäuser tells how he fainted; there is a silence. He tells how he awoke to the sound of distant hymns; we hear, softly, the 'Dresden Amen'. Again, both narrative and psychological levels are served; the musical events reflect the course of the narrative, and their non-congruence a dissolution of sanity and order. Finally, Tannhäuser collapses. He calls on Venus, and brings her up to the human world.

11. 'In repeating the steps of the criminal-predecessor, Holmes is literalizing an act that all narrative claims to perform, since narrative ever, and inevitably . . . presents itself as a repetition . . . and rehearsal of what has already happened', [Peter Brooks, *Reading for the Plot* (Oxford, 1984), p. 25.]

Tannhäuser's death is certain from the moment Venus returns. As a mortal, he cannot survive the tug-of-war between the pagan and the divine; like the Dutchman, Tannhäuser is allowed to perish in grace through the sacrifice of a pure soprano. If the last part of the opera cannot be faulted musically, in some senses its music transcends its plot. Certainly in the E♭ major chorus of Young Pilgrims [31, 30, 32], who bear the green staff and announce the miracle in Rome, Wagner invented a music of exaltation that was not to be surpassed until *Parsifal*; in fact, he borrowed a musical motif [32] from his Young Pilgrims (along with the 'Dresden Amen') for the later work.

The first intimations of Tannhäuser's death are, however, present in the Rome Narration. The anarchic musical language of its final moments is one Tannhäuser speaks here for the first time: it is the language of the underworld. In the Venusberg in Act One, he had been the erring son of human order, and had sung formally against Venus's bizarre rhetorical excesses. In the septet and in his duet with Elisabeth he is as obedient a tenor as one could imagine. But in the Song Contest he remembers, and brings into a Wartburg scene music from another time and place. Once cast out of human society he changes profoundly. During the Rome Narration and in his summons to Venus he becomes a perverted Orpheus: one who takes the lyre, sings the music of the dead, and brings up from Hades no gentle Euridice, but a powerful Goddess. Orpheus, the singer-composer who descended to Hades, is the figure of myth behind the historical figures — Tannhäuser the medieval poet, and the Minnesinger Heinrich von Ofterdingen — on whom Wagner modelled his character. Significantly, all three were singers, and all three invented music. Perhaps this is why the orchestra, and the recurring music, often seem to depict sounds, fragments of melodies, dances, and songs that exist in Tannhäuser's mind. Like all composers, he lives with an unceasing hum of internal music, and music is therefore his key to memory.

* * *

What would it have been, the *Tannhäuser* that Wagner owed the world? The notion of memory and the use of musical recurrence to symbolise it bring us back to this question. Wagner, we saw, told Cosima that he found a certain imbalance, an irreconcilability, between the older Dresden and newer Paris-Vienna sections of the opera. This is often taken to mean the 'stylistic inconsistency' between music-dramatic/amorphous/chromatic and operatic/formal/diatonic passages. Yet the opposition of styles is intimated in the Dresden version, where it already plays a metaphorical role, representing the demonic and divine forces of the drama.

But there *is* one imbalance in the final score. Though Wagner in 1860-61 greatly changed the specific musical portrayals of the Venusberg, and of Venus herself, he did not then consistently alter Tannhäuser's *recollections* of Venus elsewhere in the opera. Tannhäuser remembers and rehears the music of a Dresden Venusberg that in part no longer exists; he often fails to recall the darker, Tristanesque music of the new Venusberg. Imbalance, disproportion, something not reconciled? It is a subtle point. In a work that plays so passionately with memory and its musical representation, this subtle flaw may have lain at the heart of Wagner's final uneasiness about his score.

Thematic Guide

Many of the themes from the opera have been identified in the articles by numbers in square brackets, which refer to the themes set out in these pages. The themes are also identified by the numbers in square brackets at the corresponding points in the libretto, so that the words can be related to the musical themes.

[8]

Allegro

TANNHÄUSER   *etc.*

Praise be to   love   for   plea-sure ne-ver end - ing
Dir, tö - ne   Lob!   Die   Wun-der sei'n ge-prie - sen

[9]

Moderato   VENUS.

Sweet lov   -   er, come,   sink down be - side   me.
Ge - lieb   -   ter, komm!   Sieh' dort die   Grot - te.

[10]

VENUS

Hence to   the   cheer - less   haunts   of   men,
Hin   zu   den   kal - ten   Men - schen - flieh,

[11]

VENUS

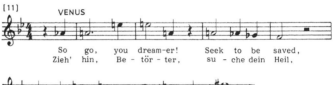

So   go,   you   dream-er!   Seek   to   be   saved,
Zieh'   hin,   Be - tör - ter,   su - che dein Heil,

seek for the   peace   you   will not   find.
su - che dein Heil,   und   find' es   nie!

[12]

VENUS   ⌐3⌐   *etc.*

How   can   I have de-served it, what ev - il   have   I   done you?
Wie   hätt'   ich das er-wor - ben, wie träf' mich solch' Ver-schul-den?

[13]

SHEPHERD

The   spring has   come from the   moun - tain - side,   to
Frau   Hol - da   kam aus   dem Berg   her - vor   zu

roam   thru'   fo - rests and   mead - ows:
zieh'n   durch   Flur   und   Au - en.

52

[14a] Moderato — PILGRIMS

To Thee I jour - ney Christ my Lord!
Zu dir wall' ich, mein Je - sus Christ!

[14b] PILGRIMS

My heav - y heart by guilt op - pressed
Ach, schwer drückt mich der Sün - den Last

[14c] PILGRIMS

And so to ___ Rome my steps I ___ trace to
Am ho - hen ___ Fest der Gnad' und ___ Huld in

più p

pray that God grant me ___ His grace:
De - mut süh'n ich mei - ne Schuld.

[15] (Allegro) WOLFRAM

N.B. No. 17

etc.

We wel - come you, oh val - iant sing - er
Ge - grüsst sei uns du küh - ner Säng - er

[16] Lento — WOLFRAM

Did mag - ic or po - et - ic muse
War's Zau - ber, war es rei - ne Macht

[17] Allegro TANNHÄUSER

Once more I see the world a - round me,
Ha, jetzt er - ken - ne ich sie wie - der,

53

[18]
Allegro   ELISABETH

Great hall of song, ___ I give you greet-ing,
Dich teu-re Hal — le, grüss' ich wie-der!

[19]
Allegro   ELISABETH AND TANNHAUSER

We praise ___ this ___ hour ___ of greet-ing,
Ge-prie - sen ___ sei ___ die Stun-de,

Scene 4 – Finale
[20a]
Allegro

[20b]
Allegro

p

[20c]
Allegro

p

[20d]
Allegro

[20e]
Moderato

tr

[21]
Cantabile   WOLFRAM

Love, pure and ho - ly, beck — on me
Dir, ho - he Lie - be, tö — ne be-

on - wards to ___ my goal. ___
-gei - stert mein ___ Ge - sang. ___

54

[22]
Adagio

ELISABETH

I pray for him, pray that he be for - giv - en!
Ich fleh' für ihn, ich fle- he für sein Le - ben!

[23]
Molto moderato

CHORUS

From heav'n an an - gel has de-scen-ded
Ein En - gel stieg aus lich - tem Ae - ther

[24]
Più moto

CHORUS

Go, join them on their jour-ney, on Rome your hopes be built.
Mit ih - nen sollst du wal - len zur Stadt der Gna-den - huld,

[25] PILGRIMS

The grace of God to — the sin-ner is giv - en, his
Der Gna - de Heil ist — dem Büs-ser be -schie-den, er

soul shall live with — the an - gels in hea - ven
geht einst ein in — der Se - li - gen Frie - den

[26]
Lento

ELISABETH

_ff_ _etc._

Al - migh - ty Vir - gin, I im - plore thee!
All - mächt'- ge Jung-frau, hör' mein Fle - hen!

[27]
Moderato

WOLFRAM

_p_ _pp_ _etc._

Look down o gen - tle eve - ning star,
O, du mein hol - der A - bend-stern,

[28]
Lento

[29]
Andante assai lento

[30]
('Dresden Amen')

[31]
Moderato YOUNG PILGRIMS

N.B. No. 32

Praise!__ Praise!__ Give praise to God in Heav'n.__
Heil!__ Heil!__ Der Gna - de Wun-der Heil!__

[32]
Moderato YOUNG PILGRIMS

For in ____ this dar - kest hour of need, the
Es tat ____ in nächt- lich heil' - ger Stund', der

Lord a won - der has de - creed.
Herr sich durch ein Wun - der kund.

56

Tannhäuser

und der Sängerkrieg auf Wartburg
(and the Song Contest on the Wartburg)

Romantic Opera in Three Acts
by Richard Wagner

English translation by Rodney Blumer

Tannhäuser was first performed in Dresden on October 19, 1845. It was revised for subsequent performances, and substantially remodelled and translated into French by E. Roche, R. Lindau and C. Nuitter*, for the Paris Opéra on March 13, 1861. This version was translated into German and given in Munich on August 1, 1867. It was further revised for performance in Vienna on November 22, 1875.

It was the first Wagner opera to be performed in America, in New York on April 4, 1876. It was first heard in Britain at Covent Garden, in Italian on May 6, 1876.

This translation was commissioned by English National Opera for a production in May 1988 which never took place. The German text is that of the 1860 published score, with additional scenes from the earlier version. The verse lay-out follows that of Wagner's published libretto, and the stage directions are literal translations of those in the libretto rather than the score.

* pen-name of Charles Truinet

CHARACTERS

Hermann *Landgrave of Thuringia*		bass
Tannhäuser		tenor
Wolfram von Eschenbach		baritone
Walter von der Vogelweide	*Knights and*	tenor
Biterolf	*minstrels*	bass
Heinrich der Schreiber		tenor
Reinmar von Zweter		bass
Elisabeth *niece of the Landgrave*		soprano
Venus		soprano
A Young Shepherd		soprano
Four Noble Pages		sopranos and altos

Noble Knights, Ladies, Older and Younger Pilgrims, Sirens, Naiads, Nymphs, Bacchantes

The Tannhäuser Ballad

translated by J.W. Thomas

I shall now begin to sing
Tannhäuser's song which tells
the strange adventures which he had
where Lady Venus dwells.

Tannhäuser was a knight who sought
adventure everywhere,
he entered Venus Mount to see
the lovely women there.

'Tannhäuser, I am fond of you,
hold that in memory,
and that you've sworn to me an oath
that you'd be true to me.'

'Dame Venus, that I did not do!
You know it's just a lie,
and if some other one said this,
God helping me, he'd die.'

'Tannhäuser, why must you lament?
Remain with me for life
and I shall give my friend to you
to be your loyal wife.'

'And if I took another wife
than her for whom I yearn,
then in the flaming fire of hell
eternally I'd burn.'

'You speak so much of flaming hell
but never felt its power:
just think about my ruby lips
which laugh at any hour.'

'I care not for your ruby lips;
they've brought me only woe.
Do honor now to womankind,
dear lady, let me go!'

'Tannhäuser, would you take your leave?
You shall not go away!
Remain with us, oh noble knight,
and let your life be gay.'

'My life grows sadder all the time;
to stay is but to grieve.
Give me permission, lady fair,
that I may take my leave.'

'Tannhäuser, do not babble so,
what are you thinking of?
Let's go into my chamber now
and play the game of love.'

'For me your love is only pain;
I've opened up my eyes
and seen in you, my lady fair,
a devil in disguise.'

'Tannhäuser, what is this you say;
am I the one you scold?
If you remain in here you'll wish
you hadn't been so bold.'

Nun wil ichs aber heben an
von dem Danheüser zu singen,
vnd was er wunders hat gethan
mit seiner fraw Venussinnen.

Danheüser was ein Ritter gut,
Wann er wolt wunder schawen,
Er wolt in fraw Venus berg
Zu andern schönen frawen.

'Herr Danheüser, ir seyt mir lieb,
Daran solt ir mir gedencken!
Ir habt mir einen aydt geschworen:
Ir wölt von mir nit wencken.'

'Fraw Venus, das enhab ich nit,
Ich wil das widersprechen,
Wann redt das yemant mer dan ir,
Got helff mirs an jm rechen!'

'Herr Danheüser, wie redt ir nun?
Ir solt bey mir beleyben;
Ich wil euch mein gespilen geben
Zu einem stetten weybe.'

'Vnd nem ich nun ein ander weyb,
Ich hab in meynem sinnen,
So müst ich in der helle glut
Auch ewigklich verbrinnen.'

'Ir sagt mir vil von der helle glut
Vnd habt es nie entpfunden;
Gedenckt an meinen rotten mundt,
Der lachet zu allen stunden.'

'Was hilffet mich ewer roter mundt?
Er ist mir gar vnmere;
Nun gebt mir vrlaub frewlein zart,
Durch aller frawen ere!'

'Herr Danheüser, wölt ir vrlaub han,
In wil euch keinen geben;
Nun beleybent, edler Danheüser,
Vnd fristet ewer leben!'

'Mein leben das ist worden kranck,
Ich mag nit lenger bleyben;
Nun gebt mir vrlaub, frewlein zart,
Von ewrem stoltzen leybe!'

'Herr Danheüser, nit redet also,
Ir thut euch nit wol besinnen;
So geen wir in ein kemerlein
Vnd spilen der edlen minnen!'

'Gebrauch ich nun ein frembdes weyb,
Ich hab in meinem sinne:
Fraw Venus, edle frawe zart,
Ir seyt ein Teüffellinne!'

'Herr Danheüser, was redt ir nün,
Das ir mich günnet schelten?
Nun solt ir lenger hierinne sein,
Ir müsstent sein dick entgelten.'

'Dame Venus, that I shall not do:
I'll never stay in here.
Maria, mother, Holy Maid,
in my distress be near!'

'Tannhäuser, you may take your leave:
though you must lend your tongue
and sing my praises through the land,
but only to the young.'

He left the mountain then behind
repentant and in grief:
'I'll go to Rome and trust the pope
to give my soul relief.

'I'll journey forth upon my way
(may God my life control)
to ask the pope who's called Urban
if he can save my soul.

'Ah, Pope, my comforter and lord,
my heart is filled with rue
because of all the wrong I've done
and now confess to you.

'With Venus I have spent a year,
a sin, as I know well.
I seek for absolution now
that I with God may dwell.'

The pope was leaning on a staff
and it was dry and dead.
'This shall have leaves ere you receive
the grace of God,' he said.

'Had I a single year to live,
I'd spend it all to win
through any penance I could do
God's pardon for my sin.'

He went forth from the city's gate
in grief and sick at heart.
'Maria, mother, Holy Maid,
from you I now must part.'

He journeyed to the mountain then
to stay eternally:
'I'll go to see my lady sweet
where God would have me be.'

'Tannhäuser, welcome once again
you've been away so long.
I welcome you, my dearest lord
and lover, fair and strong.'

The third day when he took his staff
the pope saw leaves thereon.
He sent forth men to every land
where Tannhäuser might have gone.

But he was in the mountain there
with Venus as before,
and so the pope, Urban the Fourth,
was lost forevermore.

'Fraw Venus, vnd das wil ich nit,
Ich mag nit lenger bleyben.
Maria, mutter, reyne maydt,
Nun hilff mir von den weyben!'

'Herr Danheüser, ir solt vrlaub han,
Mein lob das solt ir preysen,
Wo ir do in dem landt vmbfart.
Nembt vrlaub von dem Greysen!'

Do schiedt er wider auss dem berg
In iamer vnd in rewen:
'Ich wil gen Rom wol in die stat
Auff eines Babstes trawen.

'Nun far ich frölich auff die ban,
Got müss sein ymmer walten,
Zu einem Babst, der heyst Vrban,
Ob er mich möcht behalten.

'Ach Babst, lieber herre mein,
Ich klag euch meine sunde,
Die ich mein tag begangen hab,
Als ich euchs wil verkünde.

'Ich bin gewesen auch ein jar
Bey Venus einer frawen,
So wölt ich beycht vnd buss entpfahen,
Ob ich möcht got anschawen.'

Der Babst het ein steblein in der handt,
Das was sich also dürre:
'Als wenig es begrünen mag,
Kumpst du zu gottes hulde.'

'Nun solt ich leben nur ein jar,
Ein jar auff diser erden,
So wölt ich beycht vnd buss entpfahen
Vnd gottes trost erwerben.'

Da zog er wider auss der stat
In iamer vnd in leyden;
'Maria mutter, reyne maydt,
Muss ich nun von dir scheyden?'

Er zog do wider in den berg
Vnd ewiglich on ende:
'Ich wil zu Venus, meiner frawen zart,
Wo mich got wil hinsende.'

'Seyt got wilkumen, Danheüser,
Ich hab ewer lang entporen;
Seyt wilkumen, mein lieber herr,
Zu einem bulen ausserkoren!'

Das weret biss an den dritten tag,
Der stab hub an zu grünen,
Der Babst schicket auss in alle landt:
Wo der Danheüser wer hinkumen?

Do was er wider in den berg
Vnd het sein lieb erkoren,
Des must der vierte Babst Vrban
Auch ewiglich sein verloren.

Visions from Scene One at Bayreuth, 1892: above, 'The Rape of Europa'; below, 'Leda and the Swan'. (Royal Opera House Archives)

Overture [25, 14b, 1, 2, 3, 4, 5, 8, 9]

Act One

The Venusberg

Scene One. [1, 2, 6, 3] *The stage represents the interior of the 'Venusberg' (Hörselberg, near Eisenach). A wide grotto bending to the right in the background so that its end is invisible. From a rocky opening, through which dim daylight shines, a greenish cascade falls the whole height of the grotto, wildly foaming over the stones; from the basin which catches this water a brook flows towards the background, forming there a lake in which are seen the forms of bathing Naiads, and on its banks reclining Sirens. On both sides of the grotto, rocky projections of irregular form, overgrown with wonderful coral-like tropical vegetation. In front of a grotto opening extending upwards to the left, from which a tender rosy twilight shines, Venus lies in the foreground on a sumptuous couch; Tannhaüser half kneeling before her, with his head on her knees and his harp at his side. About the couch, reclining in graceful embrace, the three Graces. Beside and behind the couch numerous sleeping Cupids, lying over and beside each other in confusion forming a tangled coil, the children fallen asleep after boisterous play. The whole foreground is illumined by a magical rosy light shining from below, through which the emerald green of the cascade with the white of its foaming waves are clearly seen. The far background with the banks of the lake is lit by a bright blue haze like moonshine. As the curtain rises, the youths are still reclining on the high rocks with their goblets. They immediately respond to the enticing gestures of the Nymphs and hasten down to them. Around the foaming basin of the cascade the Nymphs had begun their inviting dance to draw the youths to them. They pair and mingle. Chasing, flying and seductive teasing enliven the dance. From the far background a train of Bacchantes approach, who rush in among the pairs of lovers, inviting them to wild delights. By gestures of rapturous intoxication the Bacchantes excite the lovers to increasing licence. The revellers rush together with ardent love-embraces. Satyrs and Fauns have appeared from the rocky clefts and now force themselves in their dance between the Bacchantes and the pairs of lovers. They increase the disorder by their chase of the Nymphs: the general tumult rises to the highest fury. Here, at the outbreak of the maddest frenzy, the three Graces arise in terror. They attempt to calm the rioters and to make them depart. Powerless, they fear that they themselves may be drawn into the whirl; they turn to the sleeping Cupids, wake them and drive them upwards. The Cupids flutter up like a flock of birds, separate and, occupying the whole space above in a sort of battle array, shoot down an unceasing hail of arrows on the medley below. The wounded, seized with mighty love-longings, cease the mad dance, and sink down exhausted: the Graces take charge of the wounded and endeavour, by leading the revellers in pairs, to disperse them with gentle force towards the background. There the Bacchantes, Fauns, Satyrs, Nymphs and Youths depart in different directions, pursued by the Cupids from above. An ever denser, rosy mist sinks down; in it the Cupids first vanish, then it veils the entire background, so that at last, except Venus and Tannhäuser, only the three Graces remain visible. The Graces return now to the foreground: gracefully embracing they approach Venus, telling her at the same time of the victory they have won over the wild passions of the subjects of her kingdom. The dense mist in the background divides and discloses a view of the 'Rape of Europa', who appears on the back of a white bull decked with flowers, riding through the blue sea and drawn by Tritons and Nereids.*

CHORUS OF SIRENS
(invisible)
[7, 4]

Yield to the fire	Naht euch dem Strande,
of your desire,	naht euch dem Lande,
filling the measure	wo in den Armen
to overflowing,	glühender Liebe
drowning in pleasure	selig Erwarmen
beyond all knowing.	still eure Triebe!

The rosy mist closes again, the picture vanishes and the Graces indicate by a graceful dance the mysterious meaning of the picture as a work of love. Again the mist divides and Leda, reclining upon the banks of a forest lake in soft moonlight, is seen; the swan swims towards her and hides his head caressingly on her bosom.

CHORUS OF SIRENS

Yield to the fire	Naht euch dem Strande,
of your desire!	naht euch dem Lande!

This picture also gradually fades away. The mist at length withdraws entirely and reveals the entire grotto, lonely and still. The Graces bow smiling before Venus and depart slowly towards the grotto at the side. Deepest silence. The position of Venus and Tannhäuser unchanged.

Scene Two. [6, 1] *Tannhäuser raises his head suddenly as though starting from a dream. Venus draws him back again caressingly. Tannhäuser covers his eyes with his hand as if to hold fast a vision.*

VENUS

Sweet lover, say, where are your thoughts?

Geliebter, sag, wo weilt dein Sinn?

TANNHÄUSER
(quickly)

Enough, enough!
Oh, if I could awaken . . .

Zu viel! Zu viel!
Oh, dass ich nun erwachte!

VENUS
(quietly and caressingly)

Tell me what distracts you.

Sag, was kümmert dich?

TANNHÄUSER

I dreamed as if I seemed to hear
sounds that have been so long denied.
I heard a peal of bells so joyfully ringing!
Oh, say, how long since I have heard that sound?

Im Traum war mir's als hörte ich —
was meinem Ohr so lange fremd!
als hörte ich der Glocken frohes Geläute!
Oh, sag! Wie lange hört' ich's doch nicht mehr?

VENUS
(as before)

What do you mean? What are you dreaming of?

Was fasst dich an? Wohin verlierst du dich?

TANNHÄUSER
(mournfully)

The time that I have been here,
no longer can be measured;
daytime, night-time, mean no more to me;
how long since I have felt the sunlight,
or glimpsed the stars that glimmer in the darkness;

Die Zeit, die hier ich verweil,
ich kann, sie nicht ermessen.
Tage, Monde — gibt's für mich nicht mehr,
dehn nicht mehr sehe ich die Sonne,
nicht mehr des Himmels freundliche Gestirne;

(softly)

the grass no more I see, so fresh with promise
of summer's healing warmth; the nightingale
no more I hear that sings of spring's awakening.
Am I to hear or see them nevermore?

den Halm seh ich nicht mehr, der frisch ergrünend
den neuen Sommer bringt; die Nachtigall
hör ich nicht mehr, die mir den Lenz verkünde.
Hör ich sie nie, seh ich sie niemals mehr?

VENUS
(in quiet wonder)

Ha! What is this then? What are you saying?
Have you so soon grown weary of the wonders
All my loving has shown you? Or regret
that you're made immortal by my kiss?

Have you so soon forgotten all that you

did suffer, even while you enjoy my love?

Ha! Was vernehm ich! Welche tör'ge Klage!
Bist du so bald der holden Wunder müde,
die meine Liebe dir bereitet? Oder wie?
Konnt' ein Gott zu sein so sehr dich reu'n?

Hast du so bald vergessen, wie du einst

gelitten, während jetzt hier du dich erfreust?

She rises.

My lover, sing! Sing and give thanks in your music

Mein Sänger, auf! Auf und ergreife die Harfe,

62

for love's fulfilment, with the passion in your singing	die Liebe feire, die so herrlich du besingest,
that won for you the Goddess of Love herself as slave!	dass du der Liebe Göttin selber dir gewannst!
For love that won you the highest prize on earth!	Die Liebe feire, da ihr höchster Preis dir ward!

TANNHÄUSER

Urged to a sudden resolution, he takes his harp and stands ceremoniously before Venus.

Praise be to Love for pleasure never-ending;	[8]	Dir töne Lob! Die Wunder sei'n gepriesen,
Love by whose power man's heart is set ablaze!		die deine Macht mir Glücklichem erschuf!
To love I sing, all earthly joy transcending,		Die Wonnen süss, die deiner Huld entspriessen,
and raise my voice in grateful songs of praise!		erheb' mein Lied in lautem Jubelruf!
The fruits of love my senses long to savour,		Nach Freude, ach! nach herrlichem Geniessen
my heart cries out, my reason and my thought;		verlangt' mein Herz, es dürstete mein Sinn:
once to the gods, our masters, you showed favour,		da, was nur Göttern einstens du erwiesen,
now what they knew, a mortal has been taught.		gab deine Gunst mir Sterblichem dahin.
From man's desires no god can spare me,		Doch sterblich, ach! bin ich geblieben,
and all too rich the love that you bear me;		und übergross ist mir dein Lieben.
while gods through pleasure freely range,		Wenn stets ein Gott geniessen kann,
I am a man, I yearn for change.		bin ich dem Wechsel untertan;
In joy alone lies no tomorrow:		nicht Lust allein liegt mir am Herzen,
I long to suffer in human sorrow.		aus Freuden sehn ich mich nach Schmerzen.
So from your kingdom must I flee:		Aus deinem Reiche muss ich fliehn —
From endless love, Goddess, set me free!		O Königin, Göttin! Lass mich ziehn!

VENUS

(as though awakening from a dream)

Why should I listen to this song?	Was muss ich hören! Welch ein Sang!
What tedious words you sing to me!	Welch trübem Ton verfällt dein Lied?
Has love flown that inspired you once	Wohin floh die Begeistrung dir,
to songs of joy that had no end?	die Wonnesang dir nur gebot?
Tell me, in what way have I failed to please you?	Was ist's? Worin war meine Liebe lässig?
Sweet lover, tell me how I stand accused?	Geliebter, wessen klagest du mich an?

TANNHÄUSER

(to the harp)

Praised be your love and all to you belonging,	[8]	Dank deiner Huld! Gepriesen sei dein Lieben!
and blessed be he to whom your love is shown!		Beglückt für immer, wer bei dir geweilt!
Envy the man who satisfies his longing,		Ewig beneidet, wer mit warmen Trieben
and shares the arms enjoyed by gods alone!		in deinen Armen Götterglut geteilt!
The glory of your realm the heart bewitches,		Entzückend sind die Wunder deines Reiches,
its wonders still unglimpsed by men on earth;		den Zauber aller Wonnen atm' ich hier;
beside a magic land that boasts such riches,		kein Land der weiten Erde bietet gleiches,

Heaven itself must seem of little worth.

And yet with you I love beside me,
I long for beauties still denied me,
long for the sky so clear and blue,
long for a meadow fresh with dew,
long for a songbird's carefree singing,
long for the sound of church bells
ringing.
So from your·kingdom must I flee,
From endless love, Goddess, set me
free!

was sie besitzt, scheint leicht entbehrlich
dir.
Doch ich aus diesen ros'gen Düften
verlange nach des Waldes Lüften,
nach unsres Himmels klarem Blau,
nach unsrem frischen Grün der Au,
ach unsrer Vöglein liebem Sange,
nach unsrer Glocken trautem Klange.

Aus deinem Reiche muss ich fliehn —
O Königin, Göttin! Lass mich ziehn!

VENUS
(springing up from her couch)

Deceiver! Ah, to say this in my hearing!

You dare reject the love I give so freely?
You praise it still, yet beg me set you
free?
Can pleasure freely taken fade so soon?

Treuloser? Weh? Was lässest du
mich hören?
Du wagest meine Liebe zu verhöhnen?
Du preisest sie und willst sie dennoch
fliehn?
Zum Überdruss ist mir mein Reiz
gediehn?

TANNHÄUSER

Ah, lovely Goddess, try to understand
me.
Your love is an obsession that has
trapped me.

Ach, schöne Göttin! Wolle mir nicht
zürnen!
Dein übergrosser Reiz ist's, den ich
fliehe!

VENUS

Faithless deceiver! Flatterer and
ungrateful!
You shall not go, you never will be free,
you shall not go!
No, no! Ah!

Weh dir! Verräter! Heuchler!
Undankbarer!
Ich lass dich nicht! Du darfst nicht von
mir ziehen!
Nein, nein! Ach!

TANNHÄUSER

Never was love more fervent, never
truer
than now, when I must beg you set me
free!

Nie war mein Lieben grösser, niemals
wahrer
als jetzt, da ich für ewig dich muss
fliehn!

Venus has turned away from him with a cry, hiding her face in her hands. Gradually she seeks Tannhäuser's eyes again and suddenly turns towards him with a seductive smile. At a sign from her, a magical grotto appears, to which she points.

VENUS

Sweet lover, come, sink down beside
me,
in soft surrender quench the fire;
the gift of love is mine to give you,
to satisfy your heart's desire.
Float weightless on a sea of longing,
free every limb from earthly care.
Your burning brow I'll cool with kisses,
bring your release in the passion we
share.

[2, 9] Geliebter, komm! Sieh dort die Grotte,

von ros'gen Düften mild durchwallt!
Entzücken böt' selbst einem Gotte
der süssten Freuden Aufenthalt.
Besänftigt auf dem weichsten Pfühle
flieh' deine Glieder jeder Schmerz,
dein brennend Haupt umwehe Kühle,
wonnige Glut durchschwelle dein Herz,

She seeks gently to draw him to her.

Come to my side, come follow me!
Come!

Komm, süsser Freund, komm, folge
mir! Komm!

CHORUS OF SIRENS
(invisible)

Yield to the fire!

Naht euch dem Strande!

VENUS

The sounds of lovers join me in their singing,
call you to sink down where my arms are waiting;
drink from my lips and feast on my eyelids,
suck forth a feast of love,
food of the gods above.
To ecstasy that knows no end surrender,

resign your flesh to love in all its splendour.
Loyal devotion is a Goddess's right:

at the spring she shows you, drink deep in delight.
So think again, sweetest of lovers,
will you flee?

[2] Aus holder Ferne mahnen süsse Klänge,
dass dich mein Arm in trauter Näh' umschlänge:
von meinen Lippen, aus meinen Blicken,

schlürfst du den Göttertrank,
strahlt dir der Liebesdank.
Ein Freudenfest soll unsrem Bund entstehen,
der Liebe Feier lass uns froh begehen!

Nicht sollst du ihr ein scheues Opfer weihn, —
mit der Liebe Göttin schwelge im Verein.

Sag' holder Freund, sag' mein Geliebter:
willst du fliehn?

TANNHÄUSER
(completely carried away, again grasping her harp)

Only to you, to you my life is given!

In praise of love I'll sing for ever more!

By lust for love man's heart and mind are driven,
his hopes made flesh by you whom all adore.
The fire of love that in my heart is blazing
shall burn on high for all the world to see!
Yes, out into the world your banner raising,
your loyal champion I will ever be.

[8] Stets soll nur dir, nur dir mein Lied ertönen!
Gesungen laut sei nur dein Preis von mir!
Dein süsser Reiz ist Quelle alles Schönen,
und jedes holde Wunder stammt von dir.
Die Glut, die du mir in das Herz gegossen,
als Flamme lodre hell sie dir allein!

Ja, gegen alle Welt will unverdrossen
fortan ich nun dein kühner Streiter sein.

He lets the harp drop.

Yet must I go, the world still claims me.
My life with you in slavery shames me;
for freedom, yes, my senses yearn,
for freedom, freedom, still I burn.
The world waits there to be explored,
even though death be my reward:
so from your kingdom must I flee —

from endless love, Goddess, set me free!

Doch hin muss ich zur Welt der Erden,

bei dir kann ich nur Sklave werden;
nach Freiheit doch verlangt es mich,
nach Freiheit, Freiheit dürste ich;
zu Kampf und Streite will ich stehn,
sei's auch auf Tod und Untergehn:
Drum muss aus deinem Reich ich fliehn —
O Königin, Göttin! Lass mich ziehn!

VENUS
(fiercely angry)

Then go, idle dreamer! Then go, go!
No longer can I hold you here.
Go! I set you free! So go, you dreamer!

Let what you seek be your reward!
Then go, then go!
Go to the frigid world of men,
from whose pretentious, flaccid dreams
we gods of pleasure long have fled,
here in the earth's warm sheltering womb.
So go, you dreamer, seek to be saved,

[11] Zieh hin! Wahnbetörter! Zieh hin, geh!
Verräter, sieh, nicht halt ich dich!
Flieh! Ich geb dich frei — zieh hin!
Betörter!
Was du verlangst, das sein dein Los!
Zieh hin, zieh hin!
[10] Hin zu den kalten Menschen flieh,
vor deren blödem, trübem Wahn
der Freude Götter wir entflohn
tief in der Erde wärmenden Schoss

Zieh hin, Betörter! Suche dein Heil,

65

seek for the peace you will not find!
Then come to her whom you've abandoned,
to her whom so bravely you have spurned,
and beg her for the mercy that you deny her,
beg her to forgive.
With scorn she will repay you,
a mocking laugh be your reward.

Cast out, accursed,
I can see you crawl back to me
in remorse and anguish:
'Oh, if I could but find her
whose smile was so loving,
Oh, if she would only open
the gates that lead to pleasure!'
At the doorway he stands,
hangs his head, sobs with shame,
there where once he basked in my favour.
And now he pleads
for pity, not for pleasure.
Away, begone, beggar!
Never slaves but heroes
come into my realm.

TANNHÄUSER

No, my pride spares you
this bitter victory.
You will not mock me in despair!
The man who deserts you, proud Goddess,
will nevermore return to you.

VENUS
(*with a cry*)

Ah! You never will return?
You mean it?
Ah, what have I said?
No more return?
Can I believe you?
How can I bear it?
Is my lover leaving for good?
How can I have deserved it?
What evil have I done you
that robs me of the right
to heal your wounds with love?
Am I, the queen of pleasure,
the Goddess of Desire,
alone to be denied
joy in soothing your pain?
Recall how with tears of pleasure
so longingly I listened
to songs in praise of passion
where silence so long had reigned.
Ah, say how could you ever imagine

that I'd remain indifferent if you came to me,
your soul in torment, crying for comfort?
Love in its glory
I found within your arms:
how can that make me unworthy

suche dein Heil — und find es nie!
Sie, die du siegend einst verlachtest,
die jauchzendes Mutes du verhöhnt,

nun fleh'sie an um Gnade, wo du verachtest,
jammre nun um Huld!
Dann leuchte deine Schande;
zur hellen Schmach wird dann ihr Spott!
Gebannt, verflucht,
ha! Wie seh' ich schon dich mir nah'n,
tief das Haupt zur Erde:
'Oh, fändest du sie wieder,
die einst dir gelächelt!
Ach! Öffneten sie dir wieder
die Tore ihrer Wonnen!'
Auf der Schwelle sieh' da,
ausgestreckt liegt er nun,
dort wo Freude einst ihm geflossen!

Um Mitleid fleht
er bettelnd nicht um Liebe!
Zurück! Entweich! Bettler!
Knechten nie, nur Helden
öffnet sich mein Reich.

Nein! Mein Stolz soll dir
den Jammer sparen,
mich entehrt je in nah' zu seh'n!
Der heut' von dir scheidet, o Göttin,

der kehret nie zu dir zurück!

Ha! du kehrtest nie zurück!
Wie sagt' ich?
Ha! wie sagte er?
Nie mir zurück?
Wie sollt' ich's denken?
Wie es erfassen!
Mein Geliebter ewig mich flieh'n?
Wie hätt' ich das erworben,
wie träf' mich solch' Verschulden,
dass mir die Lust geraubt
dem Trauten zu verzeih'n?
Die Königin der Liebe,
der Göttin aller Hulden,
wär' einzig dies versagt,
Trost dem Freunde zu weih'n?
Wie einst, lächelnd unter Tränen,
ich sehnsuchtsvoll dir lauschte
den stolzen Sang zu hören,
der rings so lang mir verstummt.
Oh, sag' wie könntest je du wohl wähnen,

dass ungerührt ich bliebe, dräng' zu mir einst deiner
Seele Seufzen, hört' ich dein Klagen?

Dass letzte Tröstung
in deinem Arm ich fand,
oh lass' dess' mich nicht entgelten,

to give you the comfort that you need?

(breaking out in despair)

If you do not return,
then all mankind shall know my curse!
Ever frigid and barren be
the world that I have left.
Oh stay, don't leave me,

(despairingly beseeching)

trust in the love I can give you.

verschmäh' einst auch du nicht meinen
    Trost!

Kehrst du mir nicht zurück,
so treffe Fluch die ganze Welt!
Und für ewig sei öde sie,
aus der die Göttin wieh!
O kehr', kehr' wieder!

Trau' meiner Huld, meiner Liebe!

TANNHÄUSER

The man who has escaped you,
he turns his back on love!

Wer Göttin, dir entfliehet,
flieht ewig jede Huld!

VENUS

Beware of pride when your longing
brings you back to me and to love.

Nicht wehre stolz deinem Sehnen,
wenn zurück zu mir es dich zieht.

TANNHÄUSER

I long for new experience;
your love is not enough.
Oh, try to understand me, Goddess,

(wildly)

it is death I am seeking,
and death that draws me on.

Mein Sehnen drängt zum Kampfe,
nicht such' ich Wonn' und Lust!
Ach! mögest du es fassen, Göttin!

hin zum Tod den ich suche,
zum Tode drängt es mich!

VENUS

But when death has turned you away,

when the grave closes shut in your
    face . . .

Kehr' zurück wenn der Tod selbst dich
    flieht,
wenn vor dir das Grab selbst sich
    schliesst.

TANNHÄUSER

Both death and the grave they are here
    in my heart;
through prayer and penance I shall find
    peace at last.

Den Tod, das Grab, hier im Herzen
    trag',
durch Buss' und Sühne wohl find' ich
    Ruh' für mich!

VENUS

Your prayers will not save you,
and peace will escape you:
come back to me when all hope has
    gone.

Nie ist ruh' dir beschieden,
nie findest du Frieden!
Kehr' wieder mir suchst einst du dein
    Heil!

TANNHÄUSER

All you can offer is love.
You have not the power to give what I
    seek;
my hope lies in Maria!

Göttin der Wonn' und Lust!
Nein! ach, nicht in dir find' ich Frieden
    und Ruh'!
Mein Heil liegt in Maria!

Venus disappears. The scene changes quickly.

Scene Three. *Tannhäuser, who has not changed his position, suddenly finds himself in a beautiful valley. Blue skies and bright sunshine. In the background, to the right, the Wartburg; through an opening in the valley on the left the Hörselberg is visible. To the right, halfway the height of the valley, a mountain path runs down from the direction of the Wartburg towards the foreground, where it turns aside: in the same foreground is a shrine to the Virgin, to which a slight eminence leads up. From the heights on the left is heard the sound of sheep-bells. On a high cliff sits a young shepherd with his pipe.*

SHEPHERD

The Spring has come from the
    mountain-side
to roam through forests and meadows:
I heard her sing from deep down inside

[13] Frau Holda kam aus dem Berg hervor,

zu ziehn durch Fluren und Auen;
gar süssen Klang vernahm da mein
    Ohr,

67

to free us from wintry shadows.

He plays.

I dreamed long frosty nights away
and when I woke at the break of day,
the sun was shining around me,
and May, and May had found me!
Now on my pipe I gaily play,
for May is here, the merry month of
May.

mein Auge begehrte zu schauen.

Da trämt' ich manchen holden Traum,
und als mein Aug' erschlossen kaum,
da strahlte warm die Sonnen,
der Mai, der Mai war kommen.
Nun spiel ich lustig die Schalmei,
der Mai ist da, der liebe Mai!

The song of the elder Pilgrims is heard. They are coming down the mountain path from the Wartburg. The shepherd plays on his pipe.

ELDER PILGRIMS

To Thee I journey, Christ my Lord, [14a] Zu dir wall ich, mein Jesus Christ,
in humble hope of Heaven's reward. der du des Pilgers Hoffnung bist!
To Thee, O Virgin chaste, I pray, Gelobt sei, Jungfrau süss und rein,
to grant Thy blessings on my way. der Wallfahrt wolle günstig sein!

The Shepherd, hearing the song, stops piping and listens reverently.

My heavy heart by guilt oppressed [14b] Ach, schwer drückt mich der Sünden Last,

can scarcely bear its sinful burden; kann länger sie nicht mehr ertragen;
my weary limbs shall find no rest drum will ich auch nicht Ruh noch Rast

until my soul is given pardon. und wähle gern mir Müh und Plagen.
And so to Rome my steps I trace, [14c] Am hohen Fest der Gnad und Huld
to pray that God grant me His grace: in Demut sühn ich meine Schuld;
for he who puts his faith in Heaven, gesegnet, wer im Glauben treu:
if he repent may be forgiven. er wird erlöst durch Buss und Reu.

Josephine Veasey as the Shepherd Boy at Covent Garden in 1955 (photo: Houston Rogers)

The Shepherd, as the Pilgrims reach the opposite height, calls loudly to them, waving his cap.

SHEPHERD

God speed! God speed to Rome!	Glück auf! Glück auf nach Rom!
Find time for shepherds in your prayers!	Betet für meine arme Seele!

Tannhäuser, who has stood as if rooted to the middle of the stage, sinks to his knees, violently agitated.

TANNHÄUSER

Almighty God be praised!	Allmächt'ger, dir sei Preis!
Great are the wonders of His mercy!	Gross sind die Wunder deiner Gnade.

The procession of Pilgrims turns to the left on the mountain way, passing the Virgin's statue, and so leaves the stage. The Shepherd with his pipe also disappears from the heights and to the right. The sheep-bells are heard further and further in the distance.

PILGRIMS

To Thee I journey, Christ my Lord,	[14a]	Zu dir wall ich, mein Jesus Christ,
in humble hope of Heaven's reward.		der du des Pilgers Hoffnung bist!
To Thee, O Virgin chaste, I pray,		Gelobt sei, Jungfrau süss und rein,
to grant Thy blessings on my way.		der Wallfahrt wolle günstig sein!

TANNHÄUSER
(on his knees, as though sunk in fervent prayer)

My heavy heart by guilt oppressed	[14b]	Ach, schwer drückt mich der Sünden Last,
can scarcely bear its sinful burden;		kann länger sie nicht mehr ertragen;
my weary limbs shall find no rest		drum will ich auch nicht Ruh noch Rast
until my soul is given pardon.		und wähle gern mir müh und Plagen.

Tears choke his voice. He bows his head low to the ground and seems to weep bitterly. From the back, far off, the sound of bells is heard.

PILGRIMS
(very distant)

And so to Rome my steps I trace,	[14c]	Am hohen Fest der Gnad und Huld
to pray that God grant me His grace,		in Demut sühn ich meine Schuld;
for he who puts his faith in Heaven ...		gesegnet, wer im Glauben treu!

The Pilgrims' song dies away entirely. While the sound of hunting horns from the heights on the left draws nearer and nearer, the distant chime of bells ceases.

Scene Four.

LANDGRAVE
(halfway down, seeing Tannhäuser)

Who is that man who looks as if he's praying?	Wer ist der dort im brünstigen Gebete?

WALTHER

Some penitent.	Ein Büsser wohl.

BITEROLF

But by his clothes a soldier.	Nach seiner Tracht ein Ritter.

WOLFRAM
(hastens first to Tannhäuser and recognises him)

It's Heinrich! Heinrich!	Er ist es! Er ist es!

MINSTRELS

Heinrich! Is it you?	Heinrich! Seh ich recht?

Tannhäuser, who has risen hastily in surprise, collects himself and bows mutely to the Landgrave, after casting a fleeting glance on him and on the Minstrels.

69

The valley of the Wartburg in spring, Bayreuth, 1892 (Royal Opera House Archives)

LANDGRAVE

You have come back, back into
our world once more, when in your
arrogance you left us.

Du bist es wirklich? Kehrest in
den Kreis zurück, den du in Hochmut
stolz verliessest?

BITEROLF

Say, what brings you to us whom
you abandoned?

Sag, was uns deine Wiederkehr
bedeutet?

LANDGRAVE, WALTHER, HEINRICH, REINMAR

Speak the truth!

Sag es an!

BITEROLF

Is it friendship, or the thought of
further strife?

Versöhnung? Oder gilt's erneutem
Kampf?

WALTHER

Are you our friend now, or our foe?

Nahst du als Freund uns oder Feind?

WALTHER, HEINRICH, BITEROLF, REINMAR

Our foe?

Als Feind?

WOLFRAM

Why need you ask? Is this the
face of violence?

O fraget nicht! Ist dies des
Hochmuts Miene?

He goes up to Tannhäuser in a friendly manner.

We welcome you, o valiant singer,
you have been missing from our
world too long!

[15] Gegrüsst sei uns, du kühner Sänger,
der, ach! so lang in unsrer Mitte
fehlt'!

WALTHER

Be welcome, if you come in peace.

Willkommen, wenn du friedsam nahst!

BITEROLF

Be welcome, if you come as friend.

Gegrüsst, wenn du uns Freunde nennst!

WALTHER, HEINRICH, BITEROLF, REINMAR

In peace, in peace we welcome you.

Gegrüsst! Gegrüsst sei uns!

70

LANDGRAVE

And I, too, welcome your return.
But say, where were you all this time?

So sei willkommen denn auch mir!
Sag an, wo weiltest du so lang?

TANNHÄUSER

I travelled far, through distant lands,
but never found the peace or rest I
sought. Ask not! I have no thought of
further strife, but come in peace — now
let me go my way.

Ich wanderte in weiter, weiter Fern' —
da, wo ich nimmer Rast noch Ruhe
fand. Fragt nicht! Zum Kampf mit euch
kam ich nicht her. Seid mir versöhnt
und lasst mich weiterziehn!

LANDGRAVE

No, no, once more you must rejoin our
   circle.

Nicht doch! Der unsre bist du neu
   geworden.

WALTHER

You must not leave!

Du darfst nicht ziehn.

BITEROLF

We will not let you go.

Wir lassen dich nicht fort.

WALTHER, HEINRICH, WOLFRAM, REINMAR, LANDGRAVE

Stay with us!

Bleib bei uns!

TANNHÄUSER

Leave me! Staying with you is useless;
I will not find the peace I need.
My destiny lies ever onwards,

for me there is no turning back.

Lasst mich! Mir frommet kein Verweilen,
und nimmer kann ich rastend stehn.
Mein Weg heisst mich nur vorwärts
   eilen,
und nimmer darf ich rückwärts sehn.

LANDGRAVE AND MINSTRELS

Oh, stay! With us you must remain
   here;
we none of us will let you go.
You sought us out, so why desert us,
when you have only just returned?

O bleib, bei uns sollst du verweilen,

wir lassen dich nicht von uns gehn.
Du suchtest uns, warum enteilen
nach solchem kurzen Wiedersehn?

TANNHÄUSER

I must be gone from here!

Fort! Fort von hier!

WOLFRAM
(in a loud voice)

Stay for Elisabeth!

Bleib bei Elisabeth!

TANNHÄUSER
(in violent and joyful agitation, stands as if spell-bound)

Elisabeth! Oh, power of heaven,
you call that magic name to me?

Elisabeth! O Macht des Himmels,
rufst du den süssen Namen mir?

WOLFRAM

Not as a rival did I speak that name to
   you.

Nicht sollst du Feind mich schelten,
   dass ich ihn genannt!

(to the Landgrave)

May I give him the news of the
good fortune that awaits him here?

Erlaubest du mir, Herr, dass ich
Verkünder seines Glücks ihm sei?

LANDGRAVE

Tell him the favour that his singing
   won,
and pray he has the virtue
to show that he is worthy.

Nenn ihm den Zauber, den er ausgeübt,

und Gott verleih ihm Tugend,
dass würdig er ihn löse!

When in the Hall of Song we all competed,
our songs were many a time by yours outshone,
but while as often you had been defeated,
one prize there was that you alone have won.
Did magic or did music's power [16]
inspire the beauty of your art,
when you with songs of love and loss
bewitched this trusting woman's heart?
But then, when in your pride you left us,
to all we did she closed her heart;
with sorrow she grew pale and wasted,
and in our singing took no part.
Come back to us, o valiant singer,
and join us here where you belong.
So she will come again to hear us
and so inspire us in our song.

Als du in kühnem Sange uns bestrittest,
bald siegreich gegen unsre Lieder sangst,
durch unsre Kunst Besiegung bald erlittest:
ein Preis doch war's, den du allein errangst.
War's Zauber, war es reine Macht,
durch die solch Wunder du vollbracht,
an deinen Sang voll Wonn und Leid
gebannt die tugendreichste Maid?
Denn, ach! als du uns stolz verlassen,
verschloss ihr Herz sich unsrem Lied;
wir sahen ihre Wang' erblassen,
für immer unsern Kreis sie mied.
O kehr zurück, du kühner Sänger,
dem unsren sei dein Lied nicht fern.
Den Festen fehle sie nicht länger,
aufs neue leuchte uns ihr Stern!

Rejoin us, Heinrich! Do not leave us! [16]
Discord and strife are at an end.
Once more united in our singing,
we greet you as a loyal friend!

Sei unser, Heinrich! Kehr uns wieder!
Zwietracht und Streit sei abgetan!
Vereint ertönen unsre Lieder,
und Brüder nenne uns fortan!

Come back to us, o valiant singer!
Discord and strife are at an end.

O kehr zurück, du kühner Sänger,
Zwietracht und Streit sei abgetan!

Tannhäuser, deeply moved, throws himself into Wolfram's arms, greets the Minstrels in turn and bows in heartfelt gratitude to the Landgrave.

To her! To her! Oh, take me to her now!
Once more I see the world around me, [17]
a world alive with nature's powers.
The heavens shed their warmth upon me,
the fields are glowing bright with flowers.
And Spring, alive with waking voices,
with jubilation fills the air,
while, overwhelmed with sudden longing,
my heart cries out: 'To her, to her!'
Oh, take me to her now!

Zu ihr! Zu ihr! Oh, führet mich zu ihr!
Ha, jetzt erkenne ich sie wieder,
die schöne Welt, der ich entrückt!
Der Himmel blickt auf mich hernieder,
die Fluren prangen reich geschmückt.
Der Lenz mit tausend holden Klängen
zog jubelnd in die Seele mir;
in süssem, ungestümem Drängen
ruft laut mein Herz: zu ihr, zu ihr!
O führt mich zu ihr!

He has returned, no more to leave us;
a wonder brings him to our side.
We praise the love that drew him to us
and overcame his stubborn pride.
So now when we are all assembled,
Elisabeth will join our throng,
and may the beauty of her presence
inspire our grateful hearts to song.

Er kehrt zurück, den wir verloren!
Ein Wunder hat ihn hergebracht.
Die ihm den Übermut beschworen,
gepriesen sei die holde Macht!
Nun lausche unsren Hochgesängen
von neuem der Gepriesnen Ohr!
Es tön in frohbelebten Klängen
das Lied aus jeder Brust hervor!

The whole valley now swarms with the ever-increasing train of hunters. The Landgrave and the Minstrels turn to the hunters, the Landgrave sounds his horn, loud horn calls and the baying of hounds answer him. While the Landgrave and the Minstrels mount their horses, which have been led to them from the Wartburg, the curtain falls.

Act Two

Scene One. *The curtain rises. The hall of the Minstrels in the Wartburg. In the background an open view of the court and the valley.*

ELISABETH
(enters, joyfully animated)

Great hall of song, I give you greeting,	[18] Dich, teure Halle, grüss ich wieder,
I honour you with all my heart.	froh grüss ich dich, geliebter Raum!
You ring with echoes of his singing,	In dir erwachen seine Lieder
to waken me from dismal dreams.	und wecken mich aus düstrem Traum.
Since he arose and left us,	Da er aus dir geschieden,
how empty life here seems!	wie öd erschienst du mir!
The peace I knew forsook me,	Aus mir entfloh der Frieden,
all pleasure fled from here.	die Freude zog aus dir.
But now my heart with joy is beating	Wie jetzt mein Busen hoch sich hebet,
and now your silent days are past.	so scheinst du jetzt mir stolz und hehr.
For he who filled our lives with music,	Der mich und dich so neu belebet,
he has returned at last.	nicht weilt er ferne mehr.
Great hall of song! Great hall of song!	Sei mir gegrüsst! Sei mir gegrüsst!
I give you greeting, great hall of song!	Du teure Halle, sei mir gegrüsst!

Scene Two. *Tannhäuser, led by Wolfram, enters from a staircase in the background. Elisabeth perceives Tannhäuser. He remains in the background, leaning against a wall.*

WOLFRAM
(to Tannhäuser)

She's waiting; you can speak	Dort ist sie, nahe dich ihr
here undisturbed.	ungestört!

TANNHÄUSER
(throwing himself impetuously at the feet of Elisabeth)

Elisabeth!	O Fürstin!

ELISABETH
(in timid confusion)

No! Stand up! Leave me!	Gott! Stehet auf! Lasst mich!
I should not meet you here.	Nicht darf ich Euch hier sehn!

She makes to leave.

TANNHÄUSER

Not meet? Oh, stay, and let me	Du darfst! O bleib und lass zu
kneel before you here!	deinen Füssen mich!

ELISABETH

You must not kneel	So stehet auf!
here in this hall of song where you so often	Nicht sollet hier Ihr knien, denn diese Halle
have ruled us all as king. You shall not kneel!	ist Euer Königreich. Oh, stehet auf!
Join in my thanks for this your safe return —	Nehmt meinen Dank, dass Ihr zurück-gekehrt! —
Where did your journey take you?	Wo weiltet Ihr so lange?

TANNHÄUSER
(slowly rising)

Far away	Fern von hier
through distant, distant countries; but between	in weiten, weiten Landen. Dichtes Vergessen
yesterday and today no memory remains:	hat zwischen Heut und Gestern sich gesenkt.
all recollection suddenly has vanished,	All mein Erinnern ist mir schnell geschwunden,
and only one thing can I still remember,	und nur des einen muss ich mich entsinnen,

73

that I lost every hope that I would see you,
or ever raise my eyes to yours in greeting.

dass nie mehr ich gehofft, Euch zu begrüssen,
noch je zu Euch mein Auge zu erheben.

ELISABETH

What was it, then, that brought you back to us?

Was war es dann, das Euch zurückgeführt?

TANNHÄUSER

A miracle!
An unexplained and holy wonder!

Ein Wunder war's,
ein unbegreiflich hohes Wunder!

ELISABETH
(in an outburst of joy)

If God has led you back here,
with all my heart I thank Him!

Ich preise dieses Wunder
aus meines Herzens Tiefe!

(restraining herself, in confusion)

Forgive me, I hardly know what I am saying!
I'm lost in dreams, and helpless as a child,
robbed of the will to reason with my feelings.
I scarcely know myself; oh, help me now

to solve the mystery of my heart's confusion!
When singers sang their songs here,
I proudly praised their skill and fame;
and yet their words and music
to me were just a game.
But what a strange new world of feeling awoke in me when I heard you!
At times it seemed I'd die of sorrow,

and then my heart would burst with joy,
with feelings I had not experienced,
and longings I had never known!
All simple pleasures lay behind me,

my carefree innocence had flown.
And from the day you chose to leave us,
my peace was gone and joy had fled;
the singers and the songs they sang me
all seemed so lifeless, cold and dead.
My dreams were feverish and wakeful,
my waking hours all spent in dreams;
all joy in life was taken from me:
Heinrich, what have you done to me?

Verzeiht, wenn ich nicht weiss, was ich beginne!
Im Traum bin ich und tör'ger als ein Kind,
machtlos der Macht der Wunder preisgegeben.
Fast kenn ich mich nicht mehr; oh, helfet mir,

dass ich das Rätsel meines Herzens löse!
Der Sänger klugen Weisen
lauscht' ich sonst wohl gern und viel;
ihr Singen und ihr Preisen
schien mir ein holdes Spiel.
Doch welch ein seltsam neues Leben
rief Euer Lied mir in die Brust!
Bald wollt' es mich wie Schmerz durchbeben,

bald drang's in mich wie jähe Lust.

Gefühle, die ich nie empfunden!
Verlangen, das ich nie gekannt!
Was sonst mir lieblich, war verschwunden
vor Wonnen, die noch nie genannt!
Und als Ihr nun von uns gegangen —

war Frieden mir und Lust dahin;
die Weisen, die die Sänger sangen,
erschienen matt mir, trüb ihr Sinn.
Im Traume fühlt' ich dumpfe Schmerzen,
mein Wachen ward trübsel'ger Wahn;
die Freude zog aus meinem Herzen —
Heinrich! Was tatet Ihr mir an?

TANNHÄUSER
(enraptured)

The power of love be praised for ever!
Love has inspired my song to you;
Love spoke to you through all I sang here,
and brings me to your side once more.

Den Gott der Liebe sollst du preisen,
er hat die Saiten mir berührt,
er sprach zu mir aus meinen Weisen,
zu dir hat er mich hergeführt!

ELISABETH

We praise this hour of greeting,
we praise the power of love,
that looks upon our meeting

[19] Gepriesen sei die Stunde,
gepriesen sei die Macht,
die mir so holde Kunde

74

with blessings from above!
Your heart to mine has spoken,
your spirit calls to me;
to love I have awoken,
and love has set me free!

von Eurer Näh' gebracht!
Von Wonneglanz umgeben
lacht mir der Sonne Schein;
erwacht zu neuem Leben,
nenn ich die Freude mein!

TANNHÄUSER

We praise this hour of greeting,
we praise the power of love,
that looks upon our meeting
with blessings from above.
At last the spell is broken;
new life is given to me.
To love I have awoken,
and love has set me free!

Gepriesen sei die Stunde,
gepriesen sei die Macht,
die mir so holde Kunde
aus deinem Mund gebracht.
Dem neu erkannten Leben
darf ich mich mutig weihn;
ich nenn in freud'gem Beben
sein schönstes Wunder mein!

WOLFRAM
(in the background)

My love remains unspoken,
and every hope has gone!

So flieht für dieses Leben
mir jeder Hoffnung Schein!

Tannhäuser parts from Elisabeth; he goes towards Wolfram and embraces him fervently, then disappears with him by the staircase. Elisabeth watches Tannhäuser from the balcony.

Scene Three. *The Landgrave enters from a side entrance. Elisabeth hurries to meet him, hiding her face on his breast.*

LANDGRAVE

Here in this hall, how strange to find
    you, when
so long you have been absent. Can it be
our singers' festival that tempts you
    back here?

Dich treff ich hier in dieser Halle, die
so lange du gemieden? Endlich denn
lockt dich ein Sängerfest, das wir
    bereiten?

ELISABETH

Dear uncle, more to me than father!

Mein Oheim! O mein güt'ger Vater!

LANDGRAVE

Or have you come to tell me what
your heart is hiding?

Drängt es dich, dein Herz mir
endlich zu erschliessen?

ELISABETH

How can I say it? Read in my
eyes instead.

Sieh' mir ins Auge! Sprechen kann
ich nicht.

LANDGRAVE

Then let your thoughts still be unspoken
and keep your secret close concealed,
your silence should remain unbroken
until the answer is revealed.
Enough: the magic that the power of
    music
unleashes and inspires, today we shall
discover, and with fulfilment crown it.
The word of art will be transformed to
    deed.

Noch bleibe denn unausgesprochen
dein süss Geheimnis kurze Frist;
der Zauber bleibe ungebrochen,
bis du der Lösung mächtig bist.
So sei's! Was der Gesang so
    Wunderbares
erweckt und angeregt, soll heute er
enthüllen und mit Vollendung krönen!
Die holde Kunst, sie werde jetzt zur
    Tat!

Trumpets sound in the distance, as though in the castle courtyard. [20a]

Soon you will see our countrymen
    assembled.
They have been bidden to a solemn
    feast;
greater their numbers than before, for
    they
have heard that you will crown the
    victor's brow.

Schon nahen sich die Edlen meiner
    Lande,
die ich zum seltnen Fest hieher beschied;
zahlreicher nahen sie als je, da sie
gehört, dass du des Festes Fürstin seist.

Scene Four. *The Landgrave and Elisabeth go onto the balcony to watch the arrival of the guests.*
Four pages enter and announce them. They receive commands from the Landgrave for their reception.
From here on, the Knights and Counts, with their ladies and retinue, which remains in the
background, enter singly and are received by the Landgrave and Elisabeth. [20a, b, c]

KNIGHTS, NOBLES AND LADIES

Hail noble hall where man rejoices!	Freudig begrüssen wir die edle Halle,
Here art and music shall prevail.	wo Kunst und Frieden immer nur
	verweil',
Long will we sing with joyful voices,	wo lange noch der frohe Ruf erschalle:
hail to our leader, Landgrave Hermann	Thüringens Fürsten, Landgraf Hermann
hail!	Heil!

A Count arrives, with an imposing retinue.

Hail to our leader, Landgrave Hermann	Thüringens Fürsten, Landgraf Hermann,
hail!	Heil!

The guests have all taken the places assigned them, forming a large half-circle. The Minstrels enter,
greet the assembly in stately fashion and are led to their places by the Pages. The Landgrave
rises.

LANDGRAVE

How often in the past, at this assembly,	Gar viel und schön ward hier in dieser Halle
those gathered here have heard your songs with pleasure;	von euch, ihr lieben Sänger, schon gesungen;
with simple words or parables of wisdom	in weisen Rätseln wie in heitren Liedern
you have enriched our quality of life.	erfreutet ihr gleich sinning inser Herz.
What if our swords were drawn in righteous anger,	Wenn unser Schwert in blutig ernsten Kämpfen
called to defend the safety of the state,	stritt für des deutschen Reiches Majestät,
both to repel invaders from our borders,	wenn wir dem grimmen Welfen widerstanden
and crush dissent within our nation's confines?	und dem verderbenvollen Zwiespalt wehrten:
The art of song has played its part in battle.	so ward von euch nicht mindrer Preis errungen.
For virtue and our ancient customs,	Der Anmut und der holden Sitte,
for chastity and true religion	der Tugend und dem reinen Glauben
you fought beside us with your art,	erstrittet ihr durch eure Kunst
and won a victory no less great.	gar hohen, herrlich schönen Sieg.
And so in peace we turn again to song:	Bereitet heute uns denn auch ein Fest,
today when a valiant singer has returned	heut, wo der kühne Sänger uns zurück
to us, and one whose absence all regretted.	— gekehrt, den wir so ungern lang vermissten.
What brought him back here to join our singing,	Was wieder ihn in unsre Nähe brachte,
a closely guarded secret still remains;	ein wunderbar Geheimnis dünkt es mich.
who knows, perhaps our songs today will solve it;	Durch Liedes Kunst sollt ihr es uns enthüllen,
and so this is the theme that I propose:	deshalb stell ich die Frage jetzt an euch:
sing now of love, its nature and its meaning.	könnt ihr der Liebe Wesen mir ergründen?
He who in song responds most nobly to	Wer es vermag, wer sie am würdigsten
this theme, shall by Elisabeth be crowned.	besingt, dem reich' Elisabeth den Preis,
However high the prize, let him demand it:	er fordre ihn, so hoch und kühn er wolle,
I promise on my honour she will grant it.	ich sorge, dass sie ihn gewähren solle.

76

Rise, worthy singers: tune your inspiration!
Let each man seize his chance: fight for the prize,
and for us all I thank you in advance.

Auf, liebe Sänger! Greifet in die Saiten!
Die Aufgab' ist gestellt, kämpft um den Preis
und nehmet all im voraus unsren Dank!

Fanfares. [20a]

KNIGHTS, NOBLES AND LADIES

Hail! Hail! Hail to our leader! Hail!
Protector of the nation's art!

Heil! Heil! Thüringens Fürsten Heil!
Der holden Kunst Beschützer Heil!

All seat themselves. The four Pages advance and collect from the Minstrels, one by one, in a golden cup, rolls of paper on which each has written his name: this cup they present to Elisabeth, who draws one of the papers out and hands it to the Pages, who read the name and then advance ceremoniously into the middle.

FOUR PAGES

Wolfram of Eschenbach is chosen!

Wolfram von Eschenbach, beginne!

The Pages seat themselves at the feet of the Landgrave and Elisabeth. Wolfram rises. Tannhäuser leans, as though dreaming, upon his harp.

WOLFRAM

Turning my gaze upon this proud assembly,
warmth fills my heart to see so fair a scene;
so many heroes, valiant, wise and noble,
a very forest, upright, fresh and green;

and at their side I see their virtuous ladies,
fresh as a field in spring bedecked with flowers.
All mortal eyes are dazzled by their beauty:
to hymn it lies beyond a poet's powers.

Then I look up to stars above me shining;
one holds my gaze, more than all others fair:
its radiance fills my heart with chaste devotion,
and reverently my soul sinks down in prayer.
And then I seem to see a mystic fountain,
so clear and pure, I tremble at the sight:
it is the source of every human pleasure

and fills my heart with wonder and delight.
I never could defile the fountain's beauty,
or cloud its purity with wanton deed;

in humble devotion I kneel and guard it,
this holy source of every human need.

This anthem, hear and with good heart receive it:

Blick ich umher in diesem edlen Kreise,
welch hoher Anblick macht mein Herz erglühn!
So viel der Helden, tapfer, deutsch und weise,
ein stolzer Eichwald, herrlich, frisch und grün.
Und hold und tugendsam erblick ich Frauen,
lieblicher Blüten düftereichsten Kranz.

Es wird der Blick wohl trunken mir vom Schauen,
mein Lied verstummt vor solcher Anmut Glanz.
Da blick ich auf zu einem nur der Sterne,
der an dem Himmel, der mich blendet steht:
es sammelt sich mein Geist aus jener Ferne,
andächtig sinkt die Seele in Gebet.
Und sieh! Mir zeiget sich ein Wunderbronnen,
in den mein Geist voll hohen Staunens blickt:
aus ihm er schöpfet gnadenreiche Wonnen,
durch die mein Herz er namenlos erquickt.
Und nimmer möcht ich diesen Bronnen trüben,
berühren nicht den Quell mit frevlem Mut:
in Anbetung möcht' ich mich opfernd üben,
vergiessen froh mein letztes Herzensblut.
Ihr Edlen mögt in diesen Worten lesen,

such is the world of love as I perceive it.

wie ich erkenn der Liebe reinstes Wesen!

He takes his seat.

KNIGHTS, NOBLES AND LADIES
(*applauding*)

Well sung, well sung! We like your noble song!

So ist's! So ist's! Gepriesen sei dein Lied!

*

Tannhäuser starts up as if from a dream; his defiant mien immediately changes to an expression of ecstasy as he gazes before him into the air; a slight trembling of the hand, which unconsciously seeks the strings of the harp, a sinister smile of the mouth, show that a strange spell has seized him. As he then, as though awaking, sweeps his harp-strings powerfully, his whole bearing betrays that he scarcely knows where he is, and, especially, that he is no longer conscious of Elisabeth's presence.

---

* In the Paris version the following two songs were omitted. Tannhäuser originally answered Wolfram . . .

TANNHÄUSER
(*who, towards the end of Wolfram's song seems to have been waking from a dream, rises quickly*)

I too may call myself so fortunate,
Wolfram, to see what you have seen.
Who could not know that fountain?
Hear me praise its virtues loud and long.
But I cannot approach this source
without feeling wild desire,
I must cool a burning thirst
and satisfy it with my lips.
In long draughts I draw pleasure
and will not tremble at the sight,
for just as endless as its wonders
is my desire for its delight.
So I will shake my body's longings
and I will drink both deep and long;
consider, Wolfram, love's true nature
as I reveal it in my song.

Auch ich darf mich so glücklich nennen
zu schaun, was, Wolfram, du geschaut!
Wer sollte nicht den Bronnen kennen?
Hör, seine Rugend preis ich laut!
Doch ohne Sehnsucht heiss zu fühlen
ich seinem Quell nicht nahen kann.
Des Durstes Brennen muss ich kühlen,
getrost leg ich die Lippen an.
In vollen Zügen trink ich Wonnen,
in die kein Zagen je sich mischt:
denn unversiegbar ist der Bronnen,
wie mein Verlangen nie erlischt.
So, dass mein Sehnen ewig brenne,
lab an dem Quell ich ewig mich:
und wisse, Wolfram, so erkenne
der Liebe wahrstes Wesen ich!

He sits down. Elisabeth makes a gesture to show her approval but, as the audience is silently expectant, she restrains herself.

WALTER
(*rising*)

The fountain that Wolfram has described
my airy spirit too has seen,
but you who thirst for it,
you, Heinrich, mistake its true nature.
Hear then, and learn
that this fountain is chastity itself;
you should worship it with all due fervour
and honour its pure beauty.
If you touch it with your lips
to cool your fleshly longings,
yes, even touch the very edge,
you would sully its wondrous power for ever.
If you seek refreshment from this fountain,
you must drink from it with your heart, not your lips.

Den Bronnen, den uns Wolfram nannte,
ihn schaut auch meines Geistes Licht;
doch, der in Durst für ihn entbrannte,
du, Heinrich, kennst ihn wahrlich nicht.
Lass dir denn sagen, lass dich lehren:
der Bronnen ist die Tugend wahr.
Du sollst in Inbrunst ihn verchren
und opfern seinem holden Klar.
Legst du an seinen Quell die Lippen,
zu kühlen frevle Leidenschaft,
ja, wollst du am Rand nur nippen,
wich' ewig ihm die Wunderkraft!
Willst du Erquickung aus dem Bronnen haben,
musst du dein Herz, nicht deinen Gaumen laben.

He sits down.

THE AUDIENCE
(*in singlehearted approval*)

Hail Walter! Praised be your song!

Heil Walter! Preis sei deinem Liede!

O [Walter] Wolfram, why must you mislead us:
if human love is as you say,
while we were languishing so shyly,

the world would wither and decay.
To God on high let every praise be given,
gaze up and worship your radiant star in heaven;
worship and wonder give to each,
since they are both beyond our reach.
But all that we can touch and see
excites our hearts with restless fire;
all that is flesh and blood as we are
is but an object of desire.
I will draw near your mystic fountain,

and will not tremble at the sight,
for just as endless as its wonders
is my desire for its delight.
So I will slake my body's longings
and I will drink both deep and long!
Consider, Wolfram, love's true nature,
as I extol it in my song.

[2, 1] O [Walter] Wolfram, der du also sangest,
du hast die Liebe arg entstellt!
Wenn du in solchem Schmachten bangest,
versiegte wahrlich wohl die Welt.
Zu Gottes Preis in hoch erhabne Fernen,
blickt auf zum Himmel, blickt auf zu seinen Sternen!
Anbetung solchen Wundern zollt,
da ihr sie nicht begreifen sollt!
Doch was sich der Berührung beuget,
mir Herz und Sinnen nahe liegt,
was sich, aus gleichem Stoff erzeuget
in weicher Formung an mich schmiegt —
ich nah' ihm kühn, dem Quel der Wonnen,
in die kein Zagen je sich mischt,
denn unversiegbar ist der Bronnen,
wie mein Verlangen nie erlischt:
so, dass mein Sehnen ewig brenne,
lab' an dem Quell ich ewig mich!
Und wisse, Wolfram, so erkenne
der Liebe wahrstes Wesen ich.

General astonishment. Elisabeth in a conflict of feelings of rapture and anxious surprise. Biterolf rises quickly and angrily.

We call you out to mortal combat!
What man of honour could sit still?
And should your loathsome pride permit it,
then hear me, slanderer, if you will!
When love excites my heart to action,
righteousness turns my sword to flame,
and every drop of blood within me
I'd shed to shelter love's fair name.
For womankind and woman's honour
I'd proudly fight with every foe,
but as for you and your paltry pleasures,
I find them scarcely worth a blow!

Heraus zum Kampfe mit uns allen!
Wer bliebe ruhig, hört er dich?
Wird deinem Hochmut es gefallen,
so höre, Lästrer, nun auch mich!
Wenn mich begeistert hohe Liebe,
stählt sie die Waffen mir mit Mut;
dass ewig ungeschmäht sie bliebe,
vergöss' ich stolz mein letztes Blut.
Für Frauenehr' und hohe Tugend
als Ritter kämpf ich mit dem Schwert;
doch, was Genuss beut deiner Jugend,
ist wohlfeil, keines Streiches wert.

Hail, Biterolf!   Heil, Biterolf!

Here is my sword!   Hier unser Schwert!

(with ever-increasing heat, standing up)

Ha, foolish boaster, Biterolf!
You sing of love, you surly ox?
For certain you have never known
the joys to which most men would own.
What have you felt of human pleasure?
What purpose has your life on earth?
And as for love as you describe it,
less than a blow can that be worth.

[1] Ha, tör'ger Prahler Biterolf!
Singst du von Liebe, grimmer Wolf?
Gewisslich hast du nicht gemeint,
was mir geniessenswert erscheint.
Was hast du Ärmster wohl genossen?
Dein Leben war nicht liebereich,
und was von Freuden dir entsprossen,
das galt wohl wahrlich keinen Streich!

(in the greatest excitement)

He must be silenced! Don't let him finish!

Lasst ihn nicht enden! Wehret seiner Kühnheit!

79

LANDGRAVE

(to Biterolf, who has drawn his sword)

Put up your sword! You dare to disobey me?

Zurück das Schwert! Ihr Sänger haltet Frieden!

Wolfram stands up. As he begins, the most profound quiet ensues.

WOLFRAM

O heaven, hear me I implore you,
give inspiration to my song!
Oh, let all thought of sin be banished
from this our pure and noble throng!
Love pure and holy,
beckon me onwards to my goal.
In your celestial beauty
you have possessed my soul!
You come to us from heaven,
I follow from afar:
lead me into love's kingdom,
o shining, blessed star!

O Himmel, lass dich jetzt erflehen,
gib meinem Lied der Weihe Preis!
Gebannt lass mich die Sünde sehen
aus diesem edlen, reinen Kreis!
[21] Dir, hohe Liebe, töne
begeistert mein Gesang,
die mir in Engelsschöne
tief in die Seele drang!
Du nahst als Gottgesandte,
ich folg aus holder Fern' —
so fürst du in die Lande,
wo ewig strahlt dein Stern.

Tannhäuser jumps up.

TANNHÄUSER

Goddess of love, to you my life is given, [8]

in praise of love I'll sing for evermore.

By lust for love man's heart and soul are driven,
his hopes made flesh by you whom all adore.
And blest the man who on your beauty has feasted,
for he alone knows all that love can be.

Poor mortals, who true love have never tasted,
make haste, haste to the Venusberg with me!

Dir, Göttin der Liebe, soll mein Lied ertönen!

Gesungen laut sei jetzt dein Preis von mir!

Dein süsser Reiz ist Quelle alles Schönen,
und jedes holde Wunder stammt von dir.
Wer dich mit Glut in seinen Arm geschlossen,
was Liebe ist, kennt der, nur der allein —
Armsel'ge, die ihr Liebe nie genossen,

[2] zieht hin, zieht in den Berg der Venus ein!

General disorder and horror.

ALL

Filthy blasphemer! Did you hear?
Boasting he was in Venusberg!

Ha, der Verruchte! Fliehet ihn!
Hört es! Er war im Venusberg!

NOBLE LADIES

Away! Away! Away!

Hinweg! Hinweg aus seiner Näh!

The women leave the hall in the greatest dismay and with gestures of horror. Elisabeth, who has listened to the strife among the Minstrels with growing anxiety, alone remains behind, pale, holding herself erect by one of the wooden supports of the baldachin, using her utmost strength. The Landgrave and all the Knights and Minstrels have left their seats and come together. For a long time, Tannhäuser, at the extreme left, remains as though enraptured.

WOLFRAM

Did you not hear?

Ihr habt's gehört!

LANDGRAVE, MINSTRELS AND KNIGHTS

Did you not hear? He has no shame;
proud of his sin, he dares proclaim
that he has tasted fruits of hell.
In Venusberg he chose to dwell!
Disown him! Curse him! Blasphemy!
His guilt is plain for all to see;
give infamy its just reward
and put this sinner to the sword!

Ihr habt's gehört! Sein frevler Mund
tat das Bekenntnis schrecklich kund.
Er hat der Hölle Lust geteilt,
im Venusberg hat er geweilt!
Entsetzlich! Scheusslich! Fluchenswert!
In seinem Blute netzt das Schwert!
Zum Höllenpfuhl zurückgesandt,
sei er gefemt, sei er gebannt!

80

ELISABETH
(rushing between them)

Stand back!   Haltet ein!

All stand back in the greatest surprise.

WALTHER, BITEROLF, REINMAR

How could she?   Was hör ich?

LANDGRAVE, MINSTRELS, KNIGHTS

How could she? How? How could she?	Was hör ich? Wie? Was seh ich?
Elisabeth!	Elisabeth!
A holy maiden shield this sinner?	Die keusche Jungfrau für den Sünder?

ELISABETH
(shielding Tannhäuser with her body)

Stand back! Of death itself I have no fear!	Zurück! Des Todes achte ich sonst nicht!
What are the wounds your swords could deal me,	Was ist die Wunde eures Eisens gegen
next to the deadly blow that he has struck me here?	den Todesstoss, den ich von ihm empfing?

LANDGRAVE, MINSTRELS, KNIGHTS

Elisabeth, can we believe you?	Elisabeth! Was muss ich hören?
Let not your trusting heart deceive you;	Wie liess dein Herz dich so betören,
his crime the sternest sentence,	von dem die Strafe zu beschwören,
for he has caused you great offence?	der auch so furchtbar dich verriet?

ELISABETH

Speak not of me: he must be saved!	Was liegt an mir? Doch er — sein Heil!
Would you deny his soul salvation?	Wollt ihr sein ewig Heil ihm rauben?

LANDGRAVE, MINSTRELS, KNIGHTS

Through sin he forfeits hope of heaven,	Verworfen hat er jedes Hoffen,
nowhere will he find refuge now.	niemals wird ihm des Heils Gewinn!
His crime will never be forgiven:	Des Himmels Fluch hat ihn getroffen;
the devil's mark is on his brow!	in seinen Sünden fahr er hin!

They rush again upon Tannhäuser.

ELISABETH

Stand back from him! You are not fit to judge him.	Zurück von ihm! Nicht ihr seid seine Richter!
Shame on you! Sheathe your anger with your swords:	Grausame! Werft von euch das wilde Schwert
now hear what I, his blameless victim, say,	und gebt Gehör der reinen Jungfrau Wort!
and learn through me what God Himself decrees.	Vernehmt durch mich, was Gottes Wille ist!
This man has been possessed by devils,	Der Unglücksel'ge, den gefangen
his mind bewildered by a spell.	ein furchtbar mächt'ger Zauber hält,
So, may he never hope through penance	wie, sollt' er nie zum Heil gelangen
to save his mortal soul from hell?	durch Sühn und Buss in dieser Welt?
And is your faith so surely founded	Die ihr so stark im reinen Glauben,
that you presume to cast a stone?	verkennt ihr so des Höchsten Rat?
Tell me before you dare condemn him	Wollt ihr des Sünders Hoffnung rauben,
what wrong to you he must atone?	so sagt, was euch er Leides tat?
But I, the woman so unworldly	Seht mich, die Jungfrau, deren Blute
whose trust and friendship he awoke,	mit einem jähen Schlag er brach,
I who have loved, loved him so deeply,	die ihn geleibt tief im Gemüte,
whose simple trusting heart he broke,	der jubelnd er das Herz zerstach!
I pray for him, pray that he be forgiven. [22]	Ich fleh für ihn, ich flehe für sein Leben,
Let not his hope of pardon be denied;	reuvoll zur Busse lenke er den Schritt!

81

to faith restore him, faith and trust in
    Heaven:
it was for him, too, that our Saviour
    died.

Der Mut des Glaubens sei ihm neu
    gegeben,
dass auch für ihn einst der Erlöser litt!

Little by little during Elisabeth's plea, violently excited, Tannhäuser sinks in contrition from the climax of his ecstasy and defiance.

TANNHÄUSER
In fearful desolation he falls to the floor.

God! Look down in Thy mercy!

Weh! Weh, mir Unglückel'gem!

LANDGRAVE, MINSTRELS, KNIGHTS

From Heaven an angel has descended
in this your greatest hour of need;
behold the saint you have dishonoured,
and ponder on your cruel deed.
You gave her death: she prays to us to
    save you,
begs for your life, an angel at your side;

though we ourselves would sin if we
    forgave you,
the voice of Heaven may not be denied!

[23] Ein Engel stieg aus lichtem Äther,
zu künden Gottes heil'gen Rat —
blick hin, du schändlicher Verräter,
werd inne deiner Missetat!
Du gabst ihr Tod, sie bittet für dein
    Leben;
wer bliebe rauh, hört er des Engels
    Flehn?
Darf ich auch nicht dem Schuldigen
    vergeben,
dem Himmelswort kann nicht ich
    widerstehn.

TANNHÄUSER

To save a sinner from damnation,
an angel came to guard my days,
but I, I saw her, and desired her,
soiled her with sly and lustful gaze.
O Thou, high above this vale of sorrow,
who sent this angel that I might repent,
have mercy, Lord, on one who, steeped
    in evil,
dared to profane the messenger you
    sent.
Have mercy, Lord, I cry to Thee.

Zum Heil den Sündigen zu führen,
die Gottgesandte nahte mir!
Doch, ach, sie frevelnd zu berühren,
hob ich den Lästerblick zu ihr!
O du, hoch über diesen Erdengründen,
die mir den Engel meines Heils gesandt,
erbarm dich mein, der, ach! so tief in
    Sünden,
schmachvoll des Himmels Mittlerin
    verkannt!
Erbarm dich mein! Ach, erbarm dich
    mein!

LANDGRAVE, MINSTRELS, KNIGHTS

Though we would sin if we were to
    forgive you,
through her there speaks to us the voice
    of Heaven.

Darf ich auch nicht dem Schuldigen
    vergeben,
dem Himmelswort kann nicht ich
    widerstehn.

ELISABETH

I pray for him, I pray he be forgiven.

To faith restore him, faith and trust in
    Heaven;
it was for him, too, that our Saviour
    died!

Ich fleh für ihn, ich flehe für sein
    Leben!
Der Mut des Glaubens sei ihm neu
    gegeben,
[23] dass auch für ihn einst der Erlöser litt!

The Landgrave solemnly steps into the middle.

LANDGRAVE
(*after a pause*)

A crime against good order all have
    witnessed.
Behind a mask of smooth hypocrisy,
a son of sin has crept into this hall.
We cast you from our midst; no more
    can you
remain here. Your disgrace has stained
    us all

Ein furchtbares Verbrechen ward
    begangen.
Es stahl mit heuchlerischer Larve sich
zu uns der Sünde fluchbeladner Sohn.
Wir stossen dich von uns — bei uns
    darfst du
nicht weilen; schmachbefleckt ist unser
    Herd

with shame: the wrathful eye of God
looks down
upon the roof that sheltered you too
long.
To save yourself from hellfire and
damnation,
one way alone remains: while I reject
you,
I point the way — take it, to save your
soul.
A band of many pious pilgrims
has gathered here from far and wide:
The elders have begun their journey,
the young ones rest awhile outside.
Though next to yours their sins are
trivial,
they journey far from hearth and home;
with hearts athirst for absolution,
they take the pilgrims' road to Rome.

durch dich, und dräuend blickt der
Himmel selbst
auf dieses Dach, das dich zu lang schon
birgt.
zur Rettung doch vor ewigem Verderben
steht offen dir ein Weg: von mir dich
stossend,
zeig ich ihn dir. Nütz ihn zu deinem
Heil!
[14a] Versammelt sind aus meinen Landen
bussfert'ge Pilger, stark an Zahl.
Die ältren schon voran sich wandten,
die jüngren rasten noch im Tal.
Nur un geringer Sünde willen

ihr Herz nicht Ruhe ihnen lässt,
der Busse Frommen Drang zu stillen,
ziehn sie nach Rom zum Gnadenfest.

LANDGRAVE, MINSTRELS, KNIGHTS

Go join them on their journey:
on Rome your hopes be built.
Pray there to God for mercy
and purge your soul of guilt.
Before the holy Father
your sins must be confessed,
and think not of returning
if you have not been blessed.
A stay of execution
this holy maid did win:
beware the sword of justice
if you remain in sin.
This sword surely will find you;
beware the sword of justice!

[24] Mit ihnen sollst du wallen
zur Stadt der Gnadenhuld,
im Staub dort niederfallen
und büssen deine Schuld!
Vor ihm stürz dich darnieder,
der Gottes Urteil spricht;
doch kehre nimmer wieder,
ward dir sein Segen nicht!
Musst' unsre Rache weichen,
weil sie ein Engel brach,
dies Schwert wird dich erreichen,
harrst du in Sünd und Schmach!
Dies Schwert wird dich erreichen,
harrst du in Sünd und Schmach!

ELISABETH

O God, accept this pilgrim,
turn not away Your face.
Deep though he's trapped in evil,
grant him Your heavenly grace!
To save him from damnation,
I'll pray while I have breath.
Show him the light of heaven,
at his dark hour of death.
Although I am not worthy,
all that I have I give:
my life for his I offer,
I have no will to live.

Lass hin zu dir ihn wallen,
du Gott der Gnad und Huld!
Ihn, der so tief gefallen,
vergib der Sünden Schuld!
Für ihn nur will ich flehen,
mein Leben sei Gebet;
lass ihn dein Leuchten sehen,
eh' er in Nacht vergeht!
Mit freudigem Erbeben
lass dir ein Opfer weihn!
Nimm hin, o nimm mein Leben:
ich nenn' es nicht mehr mein!

TANNHÄUSER

How will I find forgiveness,
and cleanse my soul of sin?
If God should turn against me,
no pardon can I win.
To Rome I take the journey,
and there repent afresh,
to kneel in dust and ashes,
and mortify my flesh.
Oh, bless this saintly woman,
inspired by love divine,
who, though I cruelly mocked her,
would give her life for mine!

Wie soll ich Gnade finden,
wie büssen meine Schuld?
Mein Heil sah ich entschwinden,
mich flieht des Himmels Huld!
Doch will ich büssend wallen,
zerschlagen meine Brust,
im Staube niederfallen —
Zerknirschung sei mir Lust.
Oh, dass nur er versöhnet,
der Engel meiner Not,
der sich, so frech verhöhnet,
zum Opfer doch mir bot!

CHORUS OF YOUNG PILGRIMS
(in the far distance, as though from the valley)

And so to Rome my steps I trace,	[14e] Am hohen Fest der Gnad und Huld
to pray that God grant me His grace.	in Demut sühn ich meine Schuld!
For he who puts his faith in Heaven,	Gesegnet, wer im Glauben treu:
if he repent, may be forgiven.	er wird erlöst durch Buss und Reu.

All have involuntarily modified their gestures. Elisabeth, as though again to shield Tannhäuser, had obstructed those about to attack him again. She now calls attention to the song of the Young Pilgrims. Tannhäuser's expression of passionate despair ceases; he listens to the song. A sudden ray of hope illumines him. He throws himself with convulsive vehemence at Elisabeth's feet, kisses fervently and hastily the hem of her robe and then, staggering up with intense excitement, bursts out with the cry:

TANNHÄUSER

To Rome!   Nach Rom!

ELISABETH, LANDGRAVE, MINSTRELS, KNIGHTS
(calling after him)

To Rome!   Nach Rom!
[24]
The curtain falls quickly.

Gwyneth Jones as Elisabeth at Bayreuth, 1977 (photo: Festspielleitung Bayreuth)

Act Three

Scene One. *The curtain rises.* [22] *The valley before the Wartburg as at the close of Act One. Day is declining. On a slight eminence to the right, Elisabeth lies praying before the Virgin's statue. Wolfram comes down from the wooded height on the left. He stops halfway down· as he sees Elisabeth.*

WOLFRAM

I thought that I would find her deep in prayer,	Wohl wusst' ich hier sie im Gebet zu finden,
here where I often see her when I walk through	wie ich so oft sie treffe, wenn ich einsam
the woods alone, down to the depths of the valley.	aus wald'ger Höh' mich in das Tal verirre.
The wound that he so cruelly dealt her	Den Tod, den er ihr gab, im Herzen,
still festers as she prays to save him,	dahingestreckt in brünst'gen Schmerzen,
prays for his redemption day and night:	fleht für sein Heil sie Tag und Nacht:
such is the might of selfless love!	o heil'ger Liebe ew'ge Macht!
She waits for those who took the road to Rome.	Von Rom zurück erwartet sie die Pilger.
Now Autumn's here, it's time for their return.	Schon fällt das Laub, die Heimkehr steht bevor.
Is he amongst the ones who have been blessed?	Kehrt er mit den Begnadigten zurück?
This is the question, this her prayer:	Dies ist ihr Fragen, dies ihr Flehen —
O Heaven, let her hear the answer,	ihr Heil'gen, lasst erfüllt es sehen!
and while the hurt may never heal,	Bleibt auch die Wunde ungeheilt,
grant her relief in her ordeal.	oh, würd' ihr Lindrung nur erteilt!

As he is about to go further down into the valley, he hears the song of the pilgrims and stops.

CHORUS OF ELDER PILGRIMS
(in the far distance, gradually coming nearer)

My heart grows light as I see you once more,	[25] Beglückt darf nun dich, o Heimat ich schauen
you woods and fields of the land I adore.	und grüssen froh deine lieblichen Auen;
My pilgrim's staff I lay to rest	nun lass ich ruhn den Wanderstab,
now God my journey of faith has blessed.	weil Gott getreu ich gepilgert hab.
My sins confessed, I find reward	[14b] Durch Sühn und Buss hab ich versöhnt
in true communion with the Lord.	den Herren, dem mein Herze frönt,
My guilt absolved, with blessings crowned,	der meine reu' mit Segen krönt,
to Him my grateful song shall sound.	den Herren, dem mein Lied ertönt.
The grace of God to the sinner is given,	Der Gnade Heil ist dem Büsser beschieden,
his soul shall live with the angels in Heaven.	er geht einst ein in der Seligen Frieden!
Now death and hell have lost their sting,	Vor Höll und Tod ist ihm nicht bang,
for ever songs of praise I'll sing!	drum preis ich Gott mein Leben lang.
Alleluia for evermore!	Halleluja in Ewigkeit!

During the above, the Pilgrims have come onto the stage, passed by the knoll and gone slowly down through the valley towards the back.

ELISABETH
(raising herself and listening to the song)

Is that their song? They're here! They have returned!	Dies ist ihr Sang — sie sind's, sie kehren heim!
O Heaven, show to me my task,	Ihr Heil'gen, zeigt mir jetzt mein Amt,
that I be worthy to fulfil it!	dass ich mit Würde es erfülle!

(as the song gradually grows louder)

They're here at last! That is the pious
  hymn
sung by those who have been granted
  absolution.
O Heaven, give her spirit strength
for this her moment of decision.

Die Pilger sind's — es ist die fromme
  Weise,
die der empfangnen Gnade Heil
  verkündet.
O Himmel, stärke jetzt ihr Herz
für die Entscheidung ihres Lebens!

Elisabeth, from her high standpoint, has been searching among the Pilgrims in great agitation as they pass, with sorrowful but quiet resolution. The Pilgrims go away further and further until at last they disappear by the valley opening to the right.

ELISABETH

So he has not returned.

Er kehret nicht zurück!

PILGRIMS

My heart grows light as I see you once
  more,
you woods and fields of the land I
  adore.

Beglückt darf nun dich, o Heimat, ich
  schauen
und grüssen froh deine lieblichen Auen;

(dying away)

My pilgrim's staff I lay to rest . . .

nun lass ich ruhn den Wanderstab . . .

ELISABETH
(sinking with great solemnity upon her knees)

Almighty Virgin I implore You
to show me mercy, grant my prayer.
Let me be turned to dust before You,
oh, take me from this vale of care!
Let me in death once purified
rise as an angel to Your side!

[26] Allmächt'ge Jungfrau, hör mein Flehen!
Zu dir, Gepriesne, rufe ich!
Lass mich in Staub vor dir vergehen,
oh, nimm von diesser Erde mich!
Mach, dass ich rein und engelgleich
eingehe in dein selig Reich!

If ever once I felt temptation,
or once against Your laws transgressed,
if ever sinful inclination
or worldly longing filled my breast,
I fought with them in pain and terror
to cleanse my soul of human error.

Wenn je, in tör'gem Wahn befangen,
mein Herz sich abgewandt von dir,
wenn je ein sündiges Verlangen,
ein weltlich Sehnen keimt' in mir,
so rang ich unter tausend Schmerzen,
dass ich es töt' in meinem Herzen!

But if my sins are not forgiven,

just as I am, please take me still,
that I might kneel to You in Heaven,
to hear one favour if You will:
for him I loved once, hear me pray,
let all his sins be washed away.

Doch, konnt' ich jeden fehl nicht
  büssen,
so nimm dich gnädig meiner an,
dass ich mit demutvollem Grüssen
als würd'ge Magd dir nahen kann!
um deiner Gnaden reichste Huld
nur anzuflehn für seine Schuld!

She remains for some time in devout rapture. As she slowly rises she sees Wolfram, who approaches to speak to her. She entreats him by a gesture not to do so.

WOLFRAM

Elisabeth, may I not walk beside you?   Elisabeth, dürft' ich dich nicht geleiten?
[22]

Elisabeth again expresses to him by gesture that she thanks him from her heart for his faithful love, but that her way leads to Heaven, where she has a high purpose to fulfil; he must therefore let her depart alone, and not follow her. She ascends halfway up the height and disappears gradually on the footpath leading towards the Wartburg. Wolfram, who has followed Elisabeth with his eyes for a long time, sits at the foot of the hill on the left in the valley and begins to play upon his harp.

Scene Two.

WOLFRAM

With dark foreboding, twilight spreads
  her shadows,
as in a shroud enfolds the woods and
  meadows.

Wie Todesahnung Dämmrung deckt die
  Lande,
umhüllt das Tal mit schwärzlichem
  Gewande;

The soul who would ascend towards the light	der Seele, die nach jenen Höhn verlangt,
starts out in terror through the realm of night.	vor ihrem Flug durch Nacht und Grausen bangt.
There shines a star, the fairest in the heaven;	Da scheinest du, o lieblichster der Sterne,
to guide our ways its gentle light was given,	dein sanftes Licht entsendest du der Ferne;
pierce through the darkness, part the twilight air	die nächt'ge Dämmrung teilt dein lieber Strahl,
to show the path through this night of despair.	und freundlich zeigst du den Weg aus dem Tal.

Look down, o gentle evening star,	[27] O du, mein holder Abendstern,
shine on this mortal from afar;	wohl grüss' ich immer dich so gern:
for one who never spoke his love,	vom Herzen, das sie nie verriet,
watch over her as she soars above,	grüsse sie, wenn sie vorbei dir zieht,
far from this world to Heaven ascending,	wenn sie entschwebt dem Tal der Erden,
to share with angels peace unending.	ein sel'ger Engel dort zu werden!

He remains with his eyes raised towards heaven, playing on his harp.

Scene Three. [28] *Night has fallen. Tannhäuser enters. He wears a ragged pilgrim's dress; his face is pale and haggard; he comes with faltering steps, supported by his staff.*

TANNHÄUSER
(in a faint voice)

I heard a human voice. How sad it sounded!	Ich hörte Harfenschlag — wie klang er traurig!
If it were only hers!	[2] Der kam wohl nicht von ihr.

WOLFRAM

Who are you, stranger,	Wer bist du, Pilger,
alone here in the valley?	der du so einsam wanderst?

TANNHÄUSER

Who am I?	[28] Wer ich bin?
One who knows you too well —	Kenn ich doch dich recht gut —
Wolfram's your name,	Wolfram bist du,
(mockingly)	
the smoothly practised singer.	der wohlgeübte Sanger.

WOLFRAM
(exclaiming vehemently)

Heinrich, you!	Heinrich! Du?
Why walk so far behind the others?	Was bringt dich her in diese Nähe?
Speak!	Sprich!
How dare you, still unpardoned, to set foot	Wagst du es, unentsündigt noch den Fuss
upon the soil from which you're banished?	nach dieser Gegend herzulenken?

TANNHÄUSER

Do not be afraid, I will not harm you,	Sei ausser Sorg', mein guter Sänger!
nor do I wish to join your proud companions.	Nicht such ich dich noch deiner Sippschaft einen.
(with unholy longing)	
I seek a man who knows the path I look for,	Doch such ich wen, der mir den Weg wohl zeige,
the path that once so easily I found.	[7] den Weg, den einst so wunderleicht ich fand —

WOLFRAM

What path is that?	Und welchen Weg?

TANNHÄUSER

The path to the Venusberg!	[2] Den Weg zum Venusberg!

87

WOLFRAM

Oh, blasphemy! Don't say that name to me!
Are you still tempted?

Entsetzlicher! Entweihe nicht mein Ohr!
Treibt es dich dahin?

TANNHÄUSER
(*softly*)

You must know the way . . .

Kennst du wohl den Weg?

WOLFRAM

No, never! Never would I dream of it!

Wahnsinn'ger! Grauen fasst mich, hör ich dich!

Where were you? Did you not go to Rome?

Wo warst du? Zogst du denn nicht nach Rom?

TANNHÄUSER
(*furious*)

Speak not of Rome!

Schweig mir von Rom!

WOLFRAM

And have you not been pardoned?

Warst nicht beim heil'gen Feste?

TANNHÄUSER

Speak not of that!

Schweig mir von ihm!

WOLFRAM

Then you were not?
Answer, I beg of you.

So warst du nicht?
Sag, ich beschwöre dich!

TANNHÄUSER
(*after a pause, as though remembering in painful bitterness*)

Yes, I have been in Rome . . .

Wohl war auch ich in Rom —

WOLFRAM

Then say what happened there; I am your friend
and filled with deep compassion for your fate.

So sprich! Erzähle mir, Unglücklicher!
Mich fasst ein tiefes Mitleid für dich an.

TANNHÄUSER
(*gazing long at Wolfram, touched and surprised*)

You mean that, Wolfram? That you are still my friend?

[22] Wie sagst du, Wolfram? Bist du denn nicht mein Feind?

WOLFRAM

I always was until you turned to evil.

Nie war ich es, so lang ich fromm dich wähnte!

But what became of you in Rome?

Doch sag'! Du Pilgertest nach Rom?

TANNHÄUSER

Well then,
you'll hear. You, Wolfram, shall hear my story.

Nun denn!
Hör an! Du, Wolfram, du sollst es erfahren.

He sits at the foot of the knoll. Wolfram is about to sit beside him.

Get back from me! Don't touch me! I am outcast
and accursed. Then hear, Wolfram, then hear!

Zurück von mir! Die Stätte, wo ich raste,
[28] ist verflucht. Hör an, Wolfram, hör an!

Wolfram stays standing a little distance in front of Tannhäuser. [29]

Deep in contrition, as no penitent

Inbrunst im Herzen, wie kein Büsser noch

has ever been, I took the road to Rome.

sie je gefühlt, sucht' ich den Weg nach Rom.

An angel had dispelled the sin of pride
that seeped like poison through my spirit;

Ein Engel hatte, ach! Der Sünde Stolz
dem Übermütigen entwunden:

for her sake did I seek forgiveness,
for her begged God to hear my plea,
and mingled tears of true repentance
with those that she had shed for me.

The way the heaviest laden of the
  pilgrims
took up their load seemed all too light
  to me;
as they processed along the grassy
  verges,
I struggled barefoot over thorn and
  stone;
while they refreshed their thirst at
  shady fountains,
I drank the scorching heat of sun alone;
while they were singing pious hymns to
  Heaven,
my tears and blood I offered up instead;

and when in the hospice they found rest
  and shelter,
in snow and ice I laid my weary head.

I closed my eyes to all of nature's
  beauty,
for fear my thoughts be turned away
  from duty;
with joy I bore the pain my journey
  gave me,
to dry the tears of her who prayed to
  save me.
I came to Rome at last, the holy city,

I bowed my head and prayed for
  Heaven's pity.
As daylight dawned, with bells above
  me ringing,
I heard the sound of heavenly jubilation:
my spirit shared the fervour of their
  singing,
for all proclaimed the promise of
  salvation.
Then he appeared who guards the keys
  of Heaven
and all fell in the dust before his face;

and thousands came away that day
  forgiven,
and thousands more were filled with
  heavenly grace.
Then I drew near in dirt and degradation

and I confessed with growing desperation

to evil lust and uncontrolled desires,

to longings that no penance ever stilled,

and for a respite from these raging fires

I begged to him with mortal terror
  filled.
And he to whom I prayed replied:
'You who in evil lust have dealt,

[29]

[30]

[29]

[28]

für ihn wollt' ich in Demut büssen,
das Heil erflehn, das mir verneint,
um ihm die Träne zu versüssen,
die er mir Sünder einst geweint!

Wie neben mir der schwerstbedrückte
  Pilger
die Strasse wallt', erschien mir allzu
  leicht:
betrat sein Fuss den weichen Grund
  der Wiesen,
der nackten Sohle sucht' ich Dorn und
  Stein;
liess Labung er am Quell den Mund
  geniessen,
sog ich der Sonne heisses Glühen ein;
wenn fromm zum Himmel er Gebete
  schickte,
vergoss mein Blut ich zu des Höchsten
  Preis;
als im Hospiz der Müde sich erquickte,

die Glieder bettet' ich in Schnee und
  Eis.
Verschlossnen Augs, ihr Wunder nicht
  zu schauen,
durchzog ich blind Italiens holde Auen.

Ich tat's — denn in Zerknirschung
  wollt' ich büssen,
um meines Engels Tränen zu versüssen!

Nach Rom gelangt' ich so zur heil'gen
  Stelle,
lag betend auf des Heiligtumes Schwelle.

Der Tag brach an: da läuteten die
  Glocken,
hernieder tönten himmlische Gesänge;
da jauchzt' es auf in brünstigem
  Frohlocken,
denn Gnad und Heil verhiessen sie der
  Menge.
Da sah ich ihn, durch den sich Gott
  verkündigt,
vor ihm all Volk im Staub sich
  niederliess;
und Tausenden er Gnade gab,
  entsündigt
er Tausenden sich froh erheben liess.

Da naht' auch ich, das Haupt gebeugt
  zur Erde,
klagt' ich mich an mit jammernder
  Gebärde
der bösen Lust, die meine Sinn'
  empfanden,
des Sehnens, das kein Büssen noch
  gekühlt;
und um Erlösung aus den heissen
  Banden
rief ich ihn an, von wildem Schmerz
  durchwühlt.
Und er, den so ich bat, hub an:
'Hast du so böse Lust geteilt,

you who have knocked at Satan's door,
if in the Venusberg you dwelt,
then you are damned for evermore.
Just as this staff here in my hand
never will blossom into flower,

so from the torments of the damned
to save you lies beyond my power.'
Then, crushed beneath the weight of
condemnation,
I fell unconscious. When I awoke,

I lay alone in darkness and despair,
and from afar I heard their joyful
singing.
I hated that smug and pious sound!
As they rejoiced in lying and deceit,

the light of truth blinded my tortured
soul
and terror drove me onward to my
goal.
The way lies here, here where my heart [1]
was blest
with endless love upon her glowing [2]
breast.

(in horrible ecstasy)

The world of Venus will enfold me
within the magic realm of night;
her loving arms reach out to hold me
and make my weary spirit light.

dich an der Hölle Glut entflammt,
hast du im Venusberg geweilt:
so bist nun ewig du verdammt!
Wie dieser Stab in meiner Hand
nie mehr sich schmückt mit frischen
Grün,
kann aus der Hölle heissem Brand
Erlösung nimmer dir erblühn!'
Da sank ich in Vernichtung dumpf
darnieder,
[30] die Sinne schwanden mir. Als ich
erwacht',
auf ödem Platze lagerte die Nacht,
von fern her tönten frohe Gnadenlieder.

Da ekelte mich der holde Sang —
von der Verheissung lügnerischem
Klang,
der eiseskalt mir durch die Seele schnitt,

trieb Grausen mich hinweg mit wildem
Schritt.
[1] Dahin zog's mich, wo ich der Wonn
und Lust
[2] so viel genoss an ihre warme Brust!

[9] Zu dir, Frau Venus, kehr ich wieder,
in deiner Zauber holde Nacht;
zu deinem Hof steig ich darnieder,
wo nun dein Reiz mir ewig lacht!

WOLFRAM

No more, no more, blasphemer!

Halt ein! Halt ein! Unseiliger!

TANNHÄUSER

Once long ago you came to show me,

let not my search be vain today,
For now man and his church have
cursed me,
come to me, Venus, show the way! [2, 1]

Ach, lass mich nicht vergebens
suchen —
wie leicht fand ich doch einstens dich!
Du hörst, dass mir die Menschen
fluchen —
nun, süsse Göttin, leite mich!

WOLFRAM
(in intense horror)

You lunatic, whom do you call?

Wahnsinniger, wen rufst du an?

Dark night. Thin clouds gradually shroud the scene.

TANNHÄUSER

Ha, do you not sense she is coming? [3]

Ha! Fühlest du nicht milde Lüfte?

WOLFRAM

Be still, stay here, or you are lost!

Zu mir! Es ist um dich getan!

TANNHÄUSER

And can't you tell she is near us?
The clouds begin to glow with a rosy light.
Don't you hear jubilant voices? [4]

Und atmest du nicht holde Düfte?

Hörst du nicht jubelnde Klänge?

WOLFRAM

My ears shut out their impious song!

In wildem Schauer bebt die Brust!

TANNHÄUSER
(more and more excited, the nearer the magic approaches)

A whirling band of lovers rejoices!

Das ist der Nymphen tanzende Menge!

Come on, come on with me to join the throng!	Herbei, herbei zu Wonn und Lust!

Confused movements of dancing forms become visible.

WOLFRAM

No! Pray protection from the Lord, for Satan's brood has come abroad.	Weh, böser Zauber tut sich auf! Die Hölle naht mit wildem Lauf.

TANNHÄUSER

Her presence reawakes my longing; hers is the power to set me free! Come to the world of boundless pleasure,	[5] Entzücken dringt durch meine Sinne, gewahr ich diesen Dämmerschein; dies ist das Zauberreich der Minne,

(beside himself)

the Venusberg enter with me!	im Venusberg drangen wir ein!

Venus appears in a bright, rosy light, reclining upon her couch.

[7]

VENUS

Be welcome, false, unfaithful man: what if the world pronounce its ban, and will you never be forgiven? In Venus you will find your heaven.	Willkommen, ungetreuer Mann! Schlug dich die Welt in Acht und Bann? Und findest nirgend du Erbarmen, suchst Liebe du in meinen Armen?

TANNHÄUSER

O Venus, you alone show mercy, your love, your love shall make me whole!	[5] Frau Venus, O Erbarmungreiche! Zu dir, zu dir zieht es mich hin!

WOLFRAM

Flames of perdition, nearer, nearer; you shall not have this human soul!	Zauber der Hölle, weiche, weiche! Berücke nicht des Reinen Sinn!

VENUS

Now that you come again to find me, so I forgive your foolish pride, come then, freely take your fill of pleasure, and never seek to leave my side.	Nahst du dich wieder meiner Schwelle, sei dir dein Übermut verzieh'n; ewig fliesse dir der Freuden Quelle, und nimmer sollst du von mir fliehn!

TANNHÄUSER
(tearing himself from Wolfram with wild determination)

All hope, all hope has been denied me; only in love lies my salvation!	Mein Heil, mein Heil hab ich verloren, [2] nun sei der Hölle Lust erkoren!

WOLFRAM
(firmly holding him back)

Almighty, hear your servant's cry!	Allmächt'ger, steh dem Frommen bei!

He holds Tannhäuser once more.

Heinrich, one word will set you free.	Heinrich — ein Wort, es macht dich frei: dein Heil!

VENUS
(in growing anxiety)

Oh, come!	O komm!

TANNHÄUSER
(to Wolfram)

Away, away from me!	Lass ab von mir!

VENUS

Oh, come, be mine for evermore!	O komm! Auf ewig sei nun mein!

WOLFRAM

One hope remains for your redemption!   Noch soll das Heil dir Sünder werden!

TANNHÄUSER

No, Wolfram, no, my way is clear!   [5]   Nie, Wolfram, nie! Ich muss dahin!

Tannhäuser and Wolfram struggle violently.

WOLFRAM

An angel prays for you from Heaven,   Ein Engel bat für dich auf Erden,
her intercession sets you free —   bald schwebt er segnend über dir —

VENUS

To me, to me!   Zu mir! Zu mir!

WOLFRAM

Elisabeth!   Elisabeth!

Tannhäuser, who has just torn himself free, remains suddenly as though rooted to the spot.

TANNHÄUSER

Elisabeth!   Elisabeth!

The clouds gradually darken and bright torchlight gleams through them.

CHORUS OF MEN AND MINSTRELS
(off-stage)

This mortal soul receive, O Lord,   Der Seele Heil, die nun entflohn
that from her earthly frame has flown!   dem Leib der frommen Dulderin!

WOLFRAM
(after the first line of the song, with sublime emotion)

She prays for you before the throne of   Dein Engel fleht für dich an Gottes
    God —   Thron —
and He will hear. Heinrich, you are   er wird erhört! Heinrich, du bist erlöst!
    redeemed!

VENUS
(already invisible)

Ah, I have lost him!   Weh! Mir verloren!

Venus vanishes and the mists disappear entirely. Morning dawns. From the Wartburg a funeral procession with torches comes towards the valley.

CHORUS OF MEN AND MINSTRELS

Grant her an angel's just reward: Ihr ward der Engel sel'ger Lohn,
life everlasting by Your throne.   himmlischer Freuden Hochgewinn.

WOLFRAM
(holding Tannhäuser gently in his arms)

You hear for whom they mourn?   Und hörst du diesen Sang?

TANNHÄUSER
(dying)

I hear it!   Ich höre!

Here the funeral train reaches the stage at the bottom of the valley, the elder Pilgrims in front; the Minstrels next to the open bier on which Elisabeth's body is carried; the Landgrave, Knights and Nobles follow the coffin.

CHORUS OF MEN AND MINSTRELS

Blessed be the virgin, her task is done;   Heilig die Reine, die nun vereint
High with the heavenly host may she   göttlicher Schar vor dem Ewigen steht!
    stand.

Here Wolfram makes a gesture which moves the Minstrels, as they recognise Tannhäuser, to set down the bier.

Happy the sinner, he who has won   Selig der Sünder, dem sie geweint,
hope of salvation at her hand.   dem sie des Himmels Heil erfleht!

Tannhäuser has been led by Wolfram to the bier; bending over Elisabeth's body he sinks down slowly, dying.

TANNHÄUSER

Blessed St Elisabeth, pray for my soul!   Heilige Elisabeth, bitte für mich!

He dies. All extinguish their torches by lowering them to the ground. The morning light completely illumines the scene.

YOUNG PILGRIMS

Praise, praise, give praise to God in   [31] Heil! Heil! Der Gnade Wunder Heil!
   Heaven!
Redemption to the world is given,   [30] Erlösung ward der Welt zuteil.
for in this darkest hour of need   [32] Es tat in nächtlich heil'ger Stund'
The Lord a wonder has decreed: der Herr sich durch ein Wunder kund.
the staff of which the priest did tell   Den dürren Stab in Priesters Hand
has put forth leaves of freshest green.   hat er geschmückt mit frischem Grün:
This mortal has been saved from Hell;   dem Sünder in der Hölle Brand
God of his sins has washed him clean.   soll so Erlösung neu erblühn!
Through all the land let news be   Ruft ihm es zu durch alle Land',
   brought
that God this miracle has wrought.   der durch dies Wunder Gnade fand!
High over all the Lord doth reign,   Hoch über aller Welt ist Gott,
man shall not call on Him in vain.   rund sein Erbarmen ist kein Spott!
Alleluia! Alleluia! Alleluia!   Halleluja! Halleluja! Halleluja!

LANDGRAVE, MINSTRELS, KNIGHTS, PILGRIMS
(with the utmost emotion)
[25]

The grace of God to the sinner is given,   Der Gnade Heil ward dem Büsser
                            beschieden,
his soul shall live with the angels in   nun geht er ein in der Seligen Frieden!
   Heaven!

Act Three of Wolfgang Wagner's Bayreuth production, 1987 (photo: Lauterwasser, Festspielleitung Bayreuth)

Selective Discography *by Robert Seeley*

	W. Sawallisch	*O. Gerdes*	*G. Solti*	*B. Haitink*
Conductor				
Orchestra/Opera House	**Bayreuth Festival Opera**	**Berlin German Opera**	**Vienna PO**	**Bavarian Radio SO**
Date	*1962*	*1969*	*1971*	*1985*
Hermann	J. Greindl	T. Adam	H. Sotin	K. Moll
Tannhäuser	W. Windgassen	W. Windgassen	R. Kollo	K. König
Wolfram	E. Wächter	D. Fischer-Dieskau	V. Braun	B. Weikl
Walther	G. Stolze	H. Laubenthal	W. Hollweg	S. Jerusalem
Biterolf	F. Crass	K. Hirte	M. Jungwirth	W. Groenroos
Heinrich	G. Paskuda	F. Lenz	K. Equiluz	D. Litaker
Reinmar	G. Nienstedt	H. Sotin	N. Bailey	R. Scholze
Elisabeth	A. Silja	B. Nilsson	H. Dernesch	L. Popp
Venus	G. Bumbry	B. Nilsson	C. Ludwig	W. Meier
UK LP Number	—	DG 413 300-1 (3)	Decca SET 506 (4)	EMI EX 270265-3 (3)
UK Tape Number	—	DG 413 300-4 (2)	Decca K80K43 (3)	EMI EX 270265-5 (3)
UK CD Number	Philips 420 122-2 (3)	—	Decca 414 581-2 (3)	EMI CDS 747296-8 (3)
US LP Number	—	DG 413 300-1 (3)	London OSA 1438 (4)	Angel DS 3982 (3)
US Tape Number	—	DG 413 300-4 (2)	London OSA5-1438 (3)	—
US CD Number	Philips 420 122-2 (3)	—	London 414 581-2 (3)	Angel CD 47295 (3)

Bibliography

Stewart Spencer

Wagner is uncharacteristically forthcoming on the subject of *Tannhäuser* in his prose writings. His most sustained pieces of writing on the subject are in *A Communication to My Friends* of 1851 and *On Performing 'Tannhäuser'* of 1852, both of which date from the composer's years in Zurich, which were a time of self-examination and reinterpretation of his earlier operas in the light of Ludwig Feuerbach. Both essays are available in English only in William Ashton Ellis's 8-volume translation of the Prose Works (London, 1892-1899).

Many of Wagner's epistolary utterances on *Tannhäuser* are to be found in *Selected Letters of Richard Wagner*, translated and edited by Stewart Spencer and Barry Millington (London, 1987).

Among the numerous biographies of Wagner, there are two short introductions incorporating the latest scholarship: the Master Musicians volume by Barry Millington (London, 1984; paperback 1986), and the New Grove volume by John Deathridge and Carl Dahlhaus (London, 1984). Carl Dahlhaus is also the author of *Richard Wagner's Music Dramas* (trans. Mary Whittall, Cambridge, 1979), which, like much of Dahlhaus's writing, is both brief and provocative.

One of the best accounts of Wagner's indebtedness to nineteenth-century literary traditions is Dieter Borchmeyer's *Das Theater Richard Wagners* (Stuttgart, 1982; English trans. Oxford, 1989). Borchmeyer is particularly revealing on the subject of *Tannhäuser*. The literary impact of *Tannhäuser* on European writers of the later nineteenth and twentieth centuries is explored by Raymond Furness in *Wagner and Literature* (Manchester, 1982); and the stage history of this and Wagner's other works is covered in lavish detail in Oswald Georg Bauer's *Richard Wagner: The Stage Designs and Productions from the Premières to the Present* (New York, 1983).

The medievalism of *Tannhäuser* is discussed by both Volker Mertens and Peter Wapnewski in a *Wagner Handbook*, edited by John Deathridge, Ulrich Müller and Peter Wapnewski (Stuttgart, 1987; English trans. Harvard, 1989). A useful, if idiosyncratic, introduction to the medieval Der Tanhusære is John Wesley Thomas's *Tannhäuser: Poet and Legend* (Chapel Hill, North Carolina, 1974).

Reinhard Strohm discusses the different versions of *Tannhäuser* in the 1978 Bayreuth Festival programme; and Carolyn Abbate provides a highly readable account of the events surrounding the Paris revision in her 1984 Princeton dissertation, *The 'Parisian' Tannhäuser* (available from University Microfilms International, Ann Arbor, Michigan). The best musical introduction to *Tannhäuser* remains Ernest Newman's *Wagner Nights*, now happily back in print (London, 1988).

The translation of the Tannhäuser Ballad by J.W. Thomas is reprinted from *Tannhäuser: Poet and Legend* (University of North Carolina Press, Chapel Hill 1974).

Contributors

Mike Ashman has produced *Parsifal* for Welsh National Opera and *Der fliegende Holländer* for The Royal Opera, Covent Garden, and has assisted on the Stockhausen *Licht* cycle.

Timothy McFarland is Lecturer in German at University College, London.

Carolyn Abbate is Associate Professor of Music at Princeton University, New Jersey.

Stewart Spencer is the co-editor of *Selected Letters of Richard Wagner* (London, 1987) and the editor of *Wagner*, the quarterly journal of the Wagner Society.

Rodney Blumer is the editor of *Opera*, and the translator of a number of operas including *Rusalka*, *Osud*, and *The Jacobin*.

The 1970 Munich production designed by Rudolf Heinrich (photo: Rudolf Betz)

Notes

Made in the USA
Columbia, SC
02 December 2020